Mathematics Through Play in the Early Years

Second Edition

Mathematics Through Play in the Early Years

Second Edition

Kate Tucker

Los Angeles | London | New Delhi
Singapore | Washington DC

First edition published 2005
Reprinted 2006 (twice), 2007
Second edition published 2010
Reprinted 2011 (twice), 2013

SAGE Publications Ltd
1 Oliver's Yard
55 City Road
London EC1Y 1SP

SAGE Publications Inc.
2455 Teller Road
Thousand Oaks, California 91320

SAGE Publications India Pvt Ltd
B 1/I 1 Mohan Cooperative Industrial Area
Mathura Road
New Delhi 110 044

SAGE Publications Asia-Pacific Pte Ltd
3 Church Street
#10-04 Samsung Hub
Singapore 049483

Library of Congress Control Number: 2009932737

British Library Cataloguing in Publication data

A catalogue record for this book is available from the British Library

ISBN 978-1-84860-883-2
ISBN 978-1-84860-884-9 (pbk)

Typeset by C&M Digitals (P) Ltd, Chennai, India
Printed and bound by CPI Group (UK) Ltd, Croydon, CR0 4YY
Printed on paper from sustainable resources

Contents

About the author

Trained for working with nursery and lower primary-aged children, Kate Tucker specializes in early years teaching with a particular interest in early years mathematics. She is an early years teacher at Two Moors Primary School, Tiverton, Devon where she is also Head of Foundation Stage and Key Stage 1. Kate Tucker has taught children aged three to eight for over 20 years and has written widely on early years mathematics and Foundation Stage practice. She has worked with Devon Education Services as Leading Maths Teacher, Foundation Stage Leading Maths Teacher and Leading Foundation Stage Teacher, and she has also taught the mathematics module for Early Childhood Studies B.Ed students at the University of Plymouth.

Acknowledgements

Much of this book would not have been possible without the early years children of Bickleigh-on-Exe Church of England Primary School and Two Moors Primary School, Tiverton, Devon. Members of the Family Learning Group at Two Moors Primary School have also made a valued contribution, for which I am most grateful. For this second edition, I would like to thank Roy Kerrigan for his support, Vicki Davidson for her input on parental involvement and Mia Horrell and Martin Preston for their support and interest. I would also like to thank Sue Rogers for her encouragement at the outset, Shirley Brooks for her tremendous contribution to playful mathematics, David Goode for his cooperation, Catherine Lawes for her interest in early years maths and ICT, and Vicky Viney for her drawings. Finally, my thanks go to those members of the Devon Mathematics Team who have given me opportunities to develop my own early years practice.

Foreword

Some time ago, I visited a student teacher in a reception class where I observed a group of children learning about 'length'. After a whole-class discussion about 'long things and short things' the children were sent away in groups to complete a worksheet. This consisted of a column of hand-drawn objects or things of varying lengths, for example, a snake, a pencil and a shoe. Alongside these were written the words 'long' and 'short'. The task for the children was to draw a line from each object to the correct word. After about 10 minutes I joined a small boy, aged four and new to school. I asked him how he was getting on and what he was doing. He replied 'don't know ... it's too hard'. He was clearly miserable and bored. I left the classroom wondering, what knowledge did he gain from this activity? Perhaps a feeling of failure and the view that school learning is hard? I don't wish to over-dramatise the effect of this brief snapshot of classroom life nor to be overly critical of the teacher in question. Rather I want to emphasise that in the current educational climate where practitioners are under enormous pressure to meet prescribed learning objectives and government targets, and to produce hard evidence of work undertaken, it is all too easy to lose sight of the learning needs of these young children. Perhaps most importantly, this example serves as a (painful) reminder that the activities we plan may not always achieve our intentions for children's learning. It reminds us too of the need to find appropriate ways to enable children to experience mathematics in ways which make 'human sense' (Donaldson, 1978).

Working with young children is challenging and sometimes difficult. We don't always get it right. But recent developments in the early years sector, in particular the implementation of the Early Years Foundation Stage framework (2007), offer a welcome opportunity to revisit some of the most enduring principles regarding young children's learning. First, we know that young children need to be active in their learning – hands on and brains on. Secondly, play is a key way in which young children experience the world through their interaction with materials, concepts and people. Thirdly, significant others play a vital role in helping young children to make sense of the sometimes bewildering world around them. Finally, we need to acknowledge children's active role in shaping teaching and learning experiences in the classroom and particularly in their play. We might, then, think in terms of a co-constructed pedagogy as a negotiated space, based on a reciprocal relationship between children and their educators (Rogers and Evans, 2008). These principles are underpinned by many decades of robust research and inform the ideas presented here in this book in its welcome second edition. Drawing on the most up-to-date reviews of research and practice in primary and early years education, Kate Tucker argues persuasively throughout the book against the 'worksheet driven' culture in schools and asks us to consider instead more creative and active ways to nurture children's early mathematical understanding. In light of renewed interest in the play, the book promotes a play-based approach to the teaching of mathematics; one that is both appropriate to the learning needs of young children and, importantly for practitioners that meets curriculum requirements. It is especially good to see that the book acknowledges the potential problem of transition from the Foundation Stage to Key Stage 1, including a consideration of the vexed issue of teaching mixed-aged classes. Here she argues against a watered-down National Numeracy Strategy for children in reception in favour of an active play-based approach for all. This is illustrated through the many practical examples and ideas designed to help practitioners to move beyond the worksheet to more creative interpretations of the curriculum. Play is at the heart of this, sometimes initiated by the child and sometimes a collaborative endeavour between child and adult. This reciprocal relationship is vital, Kate argues, if we want children to learn in a meaningful and lasting way and make connections with other areas of knowledge and understanding. We are reminded also of the Reggio Emilia approach, where mathematics is but one of the so-called 'hundred languages' of children (Edwards, 1998). The present book conveys the message that providing children with opportunities to record their mathematical knowledge and understanding through a variety of media and forms of representation will help them to make personally meaningful connections with other areas of knowledge and show practitioners what they know in authentic ways.

At a time when the Early Years workforce is both expanding and becoming more diverse, practitioners in all settings and at all stages of their training will find this book a highly accessible and useful read. It is packed with ideas based on sound knowledge about how young children learn best. And the strength of this book is that it is firmly grounded in real classrooms with real children: it is worth noting that the ideas in the book are tried and tested in the author's classroom. I have been privileged on many occasions to visit Kate's classroom and have observed at first hand the many benefits to the children of learning mathematics through playful activities, not least the sense of fun and enjoyment it engenders.

Finally, as more four-year-olds than ever are placed in primary school classrooms (Rogers and Rose, 2007) it is imperative that young children receive experiences that capture and nurture their natural curiosity and motivation to learn. Young children are powerful, creative and competent, and we must capitalize on this in our teaching. This book will certainly help practitioners to have courage to move beyond the 'worksheet' into more exciting and creative mathematical territory for both themselves and the children.

Dr Sue Rogers,
Institute of Education,
London

References

Donaldson, M. (1978) *Children's Minds*. London: Fontana.

Edwards, C., Gandini, L. and Forman, G. (1998) *The Hundred Languages of Children: The Reggio Emilia Approach*, 2nd Edition. London: Ablex Publishing.

DfES (2007) *Statutory Framework for the Early Years Foundation Stage*. Nottingham: Department for Education and Skills.

Rogers, S. and Evans, J. (2008) *Inside Role Play in Early Childhood Education: Researching Children's Perspectives*. London: Routledge.

Rogers, S. and Rose, J. (2007) Ready for Reception? The advantages and disadvantages of single-point entry to school, *Early Years*, 27, 1, pp. 47–63.

Introduction

The first edition of this book arose out of practitioners' desire to develop playful, creative practice consistent with the *Curriculum Guidance for the Foundation Stage* (QCA, 2000), but which also acknowledged the learning objectives of the *National Numeracy Strategy* (DfEE, 1999) and the perceived demands and rigours of its advisory three-part lesson. It seemed that the Foundation Stage, a distinct phase of play-based education from age three to the end of Reception, did not appear to sit well with the previously implemented National Curriculum and the National Numeracy Strategy. Teachers of mixed aged early years classes and those teaching Year 1 children were aware that the transition from Foundation Stage to a more subject-specific Year 1 seemed disjointed, bewildering and potentially detrimental (Ofsted, 2004).

Since the first edition we have seen the merging of the *Curriculum Guidance for the Foundation Stage* (QCA, 2000) and *Birth to Three Matters* (DfES, 2002) to create The Early Years Foundation Stage (EYFS), the introduction of the Primary National Strategy (PNS), along with the Curriculum for Excellence in Scotland and the Foundation Phase in Wales. Play is endorsed by all. The *Independent Review of Mathematics Teaching in Early Years Settings and Primary Schools* (DCSF, 2008), led by Sir Peter Williams, described play as a feature of effective early years pedagogy and stressed the importance of connection-making, creative recording and mark-making and appropriate transition from Foundation Stage to Year 1. All of these features, key themes to the first edition, have been endorsed by the *Independent Review of the Primary Curriculum: Final Report* (Rose, 2009). In addition to these themes, this second edition discusses mathematical mark-making as a precursor to standard mathematical recording, highlights the significant role parents play in their child's mathematical education and discusses the positive impact it has on a child's learning (DCSF, 2008; Desforges, 2003; DfES, 2007). A learning environment which stimulates and supports independent mathematical activity continues to be a significant feature of this edition. The *Statutory Framework for the Early Years Foundation Stage* (DCSF, 2007), the *Framework for Children's Learning for 3- to 7-year-olds in Wales* (WAG, 2008) and *A curriculum for excellence: building the curriculum 2. Active Learning in the Early Years* (SE, 2007) all endorse the provision of a rich, challenging learning environment which promotes autonomy and enquiry, allowing children to practise, refine and consolidate mathematical skills and vocabulary. This alone, however, will not extend a child's mathematical development. Children also need to be involved in systematic, focused teaching in small groups where adults are actively teaching (Siraj-Blatchford et al., 2002). This ensures frequent, repeated and appropriate experiences, made all the more effective if the teachers have good subject knowledge themselves (DCSF, 2008; Gifford, 2008). What young children need, then, is independent mathematical play and focused teaching in playful contexts by informed adults who can plan for the essential progression of skills. Gifford suggests:

> An early years mathematics pedagogy combines a mathematically rich environment with mathematically knowledgeable and playful teachers. (2008: 224)

The purpose of this book, therefore, is to support this 'early years mathematical pedagogy' by suggesting activities, ideas and resources which promote playful contexts for mathematical learning and, importantly, to direct readers to texts which will extend and consolidate their own subject knowledge of mathematics and their understanding of play.

The aims of this book are to:

- offer practical suggestions to enable a smooth transition from Foundation Stage into Key Stage 1

- support practitioners in implementing mathematical mark-making in their settings and schools by including examples of mathematical graphics stimulated by playful activity

- suggest thematic links and connections with other areas of learning while making reference to the Early Learning Goals (ELGs) in the Foundation Stage, and the mathematics learning objectives of the PNS

- provide guidance on planning for class mathematics sessions, for focused group teaching and for independent play. All are based on popular early years themes and can be adapted to other ideas

- provide guidance, including some photocopiable material, to help plan and assess independent play

- suggest further reading to extend the reader's mathematical subject knowledge and understanding of play

- provide practical ideas on how to involve parents in playful mathematics education.

Owing to its practical nature, the book is relevant to all early years practitioners, but it is particularly relevant for those working in Reception classes, mixed Reception and Key Stage 1 classes, and all those addressing transition from Foundation Stage to Key Stage 1. The table 'Year groups and corresponding ages' (at the end of this introduction) details the correlation of children's ages to year groups mentioned in the book. The book uses the inclusive term 'practitioner' to refer to the broad range of professionals who work in early years settings and in statutory schooling, while the term 'parent' also includes carers and those with parental responsibility. The book is organized so that:

- Chapter 1 outlines why play and creativity are important in all early years education, their place in the PNS and their significance in the transition from Foundation Stage to Key Stage 1.

- Chapter 2 gives practical suggestions for creating and using a mathematical environment, both inside and outdoors and shows how links between areas of learning can be made.

- Chapter 3 discusses the importance of mathematical graphics and includes several examples stimulated by playful activity.

- Chapter 4 focuses on counting and using number. Its examples of focused teaching activities and of independent play are based on the theme of 'the farm'.

- Chapter 5 provides ideas for teaching pattern, its practical examples being based on the theme of 'clothes'.

- Chapter 6 focuses on shape and space and the use of ICT, with practical examples related to the theme of 'the street'.

- Chapter 7 gives practical ideas about length, weight, area and perimeter, volume and capacity, and time as aspects of measurement. The stimulus for practical examples is 'pets'.

- Chapter 8 provides exemplars of class mathematics session plans along with practical suggestions, including some photocopiable material, to help with planning, organizing and assessing independent play.

- Chapter 9 details a range of ideas and strategies for involving parents in their child's early years mathematics education.

- A glossary gives an explanation of terms and abbreviations.

- A resources section lists the storybooks, websites and resources mentioned in the book.

Year groups and corresponding ages

Age	School Year	
	England and Wales	Scotland
	Foundation Stage	
3–4	Nursery FS1	
4–5	Reception FS2	Primary 1
5–6	Year 1	Primary 2
6–7	Year 2	Primary 3

1

Why play?

This chapter covers:

- the importance of play in young children's learning
- how some theories of play have influenced early years mathematics education
- the significance of meaningful, creative contexts for mathematical development
- the balance between focused teaching and independent activities
- a discussion of an appropriate structure for a playful early years mathematics session.

Young children observe and participate in many mathematical events well before they begin nursery or statutory schooling. Through day-to-day tasks, they are operating in rich mathematical contexts which introduce them to mathematical concepts and skills. One of the most powerful, self-motivating contexts for mathematics in the home and daycare settings is play, and thus it can provide a meaningful link with school.

Play is undoubtedly enjoyable for young children owing to the freedom it facilitates, the sense of ownership it affords, and the self-esteem it promotes. Through play, children can repeat, rehearse and refine skills, displaying what they do know and practising what they are beginning to understand. Its disparate nature, however, makes it difficult to define and research has focused on a variety of aspects in different contexts (Bennett et al., 1997). Indeed, Bruce (1991) argues that 'play' is too broad a term and proposes 12 features by which to define 'free-flow' play – in her view, play in its purest form. Some theories of play, however, have had particular impact on the teaching of mathematics.

Piaget

Piaget's constructivist theory (cited in Lindon, 2001) states that active learning, first-hand experience and motivation are the catalysts for cognitive development. Learning develops through clearly defined ages and stages – a continuum from functional play, through symbolic play to play with rules. Piaget's theories have not only influenced early years practitioners in their practice of allowing children self-choice, but they have also been very influential on commercial maths schemes which assume a hierarchical view of mathematical development, and which emphasize pre-number skills, such as matching and sorting.

Vygotsky

Vygotsky (1978), unlike Piaget, emphasizes the significance of social interaction, in particular the use of language, which assists learning and development. His social constructivist theory regards social interaction with peers and adults, through which children can make sense of their world and create meaning from shared experiences, as crucial. Learning occurs in the 'zone of proximal development', which represents the difference between what the child actually knows and what the child can learn with the assistance of a 'more knowledgeable other'. Play with others, whether peers or adults, can therefore provide these 'zones' because of the meaningful and motivating social context in which they occur. His influence on mathematics has been to encourage mathematics teaching to be related to the child's own experiences and to encourage talk about mathematics.

Bruner

Like Vygotsky, Bruner (1991) shares social constructivist theories which highlight the significance of interaction with others. Play serves as a vehicle for socialization and its contexts enable children to learn about rules, roles and friendships. The practitioner is proactive in creating interesting and challenging environments and in providing quality interactions, which act as a 'scaffold' for children's learning. He advocates a 'spiral curriculum' (cited in Lindon, 2001) where children revisit play materials and activities over time, using them differently at each encounter as their increased development dictates. The structure of the National Numeracy Strategy (DfEE, 1999), with its repeated visits to specific learning objectives each half term, reflected the need for children to revisit ideas in order to consolidate their learning and move on to the next stage of their mathematical development.

Smilansky and Shefatya

There is substantial evidence for the benefits of socio-dramatic play, essentially owing to its dominance as a form of play in early childhood (Bennett et al., 1997). Smilansky and Shefatya (cited in Kitson, 1994) define socio-dramatic play as requiring interaction, communication and cooperation, which allow children to test out ideas and concepts, unlike dramatic play, where the child may play alone. Smilansky and Shefatya suggest that enriched learning comes from the adult working alongside children in their play and in fact 'play tutoring'. Kitson writes of this type of play: 'Fantasy play acts as a way of unifying experiences, knowledge and understanding, helping the child to discover links between individual components' (1994: 91). Through play, children can assimilate information into what they do know, and practise and prepare for situations they as yet do not. By selecting different role-play areas, practitioners can give access to different and appropriate areas of learning. This is a common approach in many early years settings where the practitioner will establish a cafe or shop, for example, in the role-play area to provide a context for developing an understanding of specific mathematical concepts, often those involving the use of money.

Both the *Independent Review of Mathematics Teaching in Early Years Settings and Primary Schools* (DCSF, 2008) and the *Independent Review of the Primary Curriculum: Final Report* (Rose, 2009) argue that play is far from trivial, but is a feature of effective early years pedagogy. Both reviews, the EYFS, Foundation Phase in Wales and Curriculum for Excellence in Scotland advocate play that is a mix of child-initiated and adult-supported. Adult-supported play and adult-led activity are most effective

Photo 1.1   A practitioner in role supporting children in their role play.

when embedded in a creative context where children can make connections with other experiences, and in which they are thinking, talking and are purposeful. If play is valued and there is quality adult involvement, it can enhance learning and contribute to the raising of standards (Bennett et al., 1997; Moyles, 1994). It is this involvement of adults, through skilled interactions in play, that children can demonstrate:

- improved verbal skills

- social skills

- creativity

- problem-solving and divergent-thinking skills. (Bennett et al., 1997)

Indeed, Gura (1992) found that children who played with a sensitive adult in a child–adult partnership were not only assisted well and able to move on to the next stage of their development, but they adopted this way of working themselves with their peers, reproducing this assisted model of learning.

In order to support mathematical development, all play needs quality adult involvement at some level. Children will benefit from practitioner-initiated play (or structured play), and child-initiated play, and indeed a balance of both is desirable (Fisher, 2002; Pound, 1999). Griffiths (1994) argues that play and maths are very useful partners and that learning maths through play offers several advantages in that it:

- has a purpose (it is fun)

- is set within a meaningful context

- gives the child responsibility and control

- provides time to repeat, practise and gain mastery

- is a practical activity, avoiding emphasis on written outcomes.

This, she concludes, enables the child to perceive that maths can be useful, enjoyable, sociable and cooperative, and is a significant aspect of the real world.

Play, therefore, has several important functions in mathematical development as it promotes an understanding of the cultural role of maths and the varied activities in which it has a significant part. Practitioners do not provide stimulating mathematical activities in play trays, for example, just because they promote mathematical learning, but because they are rich learning contexts where children can reflect on previous experience and consolidate current learning (Pound, 1999). Indeed, Lewis (cited in Pound, 1999) suggests that during quality play, children are:

- making decisions

- imagining

- reasoning

- predicting

- planning

- experimenting with strategies

- recording.

All of these processes, integral to play, are also essential for mathematical thinking.

Making meaning and connections

Frequently, when young children begin formal schooling, they lose interest and confidence in their mathematical abilities, often because their experience of mathematics has gone from the meaningful to the abstract very quickly (Gardener, 1993, cited in Pound, 1999; Tucker, 2003). Prescriptive worksheets and unfamiliar formal mathematical language hold little meaning for them and therefore they may struggle to understand. While Donaldson (1978) has described how young children interpret their activities so that they make 'human sense' of what they do and hear, Hughes (1986) showed that young children may have a good capacity for number, but that they might only demonstrate this in meaningful contexts. Allowing children to make connections between experiences is vital and this connection-making is not supported by the doing of worksheets. Young children may therefore find it difficult to bridge the gap between their experience of mathematical events prior to starting school, and 'school' mathematics. The early years practitioner, therefore, needs to provide experiences through which children can make connections with what they know, and new mathematical experiences and language by modelling appropriate mathematical vocabulary and symbols during daily routines and activities, such as:

- counting the lunch preferences for the day, finding the most and least popular preference and the difference between the two

- finding how many more (or fewer) children are at school today than yesterday

- making sure there are enough pieces of fruit for everyone at snack time

- writing numerals and algorithms in role play when it arises and encouraging children to 'have a go' in this unthreatening context.

If children are given a message that mathematics is not concerned with the real world, but only with worksheets in 'lessons', then their understanding of algorithms and symbols will not go beyond the context in which it is taught (Worthington and Carruthers, 2003). Both the *Independent Review of Mathematics Teaching in Early Years Settings and Primary Schools* (DCSF, 2008) and the PNS firmly advocate that mathematical learning should make links with other learning and experience in order for the mathematics to make sense and to foster creative thinking.

Not only do children need to make sense of the connections between mathematics and the real world, but they should be able to make connections between the aspects of mathematics that bind the mathematical activity itself. Haylock and Cockburn (2003) argue that in order to understand mathematical concepts of number and number operations, for example, children must build up a network of connections between four types of mathematical experience: manipulating concrete objects, symbols, language and pictures:

> … when we encounter some new experience there is a sense in which we understand it if we can connect it to previous experience, or, better, to a network of previously connected experiences. (Haylock and Cockburn, 2003: 3)

This connection-making between images, words and symbols at an early stage will often help children avoid misconceptions at a later stage (Gersten et al., 2005). Play situations can provide the very context in which mathematical vocabulary and symbols can be successfully introduced and practised by the children, enabling them to understand this more easily later on.

 Principles into practice

Context: Bakery role play

Prompt: There are five buns on the shelf today. Can you make a record for the baker to show how many have been sold and how many are left?

(Continued)

> *(Continued)*
>
> The children will have opportunities to:
>
> - 'sell' the buns (manipulate concrete objects)
> - talk about the experience with peers and adults using the language of number and subtraction (use mathematical language)
> - move the buns (create an image or picture)
> - record responses using their own graphics or standard notation (use symbols and/or pictures).

Play and creativity

Creativity can be considered to be the key component of all young children's learning. Indeed, it is central to the philosophy of the Italian Reggio Emilia approach to education. Although difficult to define, creativity essentially comprises four main aspects: imagination, purpose, originality and value (NACCCE, 1999). Fawcett (2002) develops a definition specifically for young children, suggesting that youngsters are likely to be creative when they:

- show curiosity

- use ideas and experiences

- make new connections through play

- evaluate the process.

Children will be creative when they are involved in well-planned play and when time is given for them to review and evaluate their experience. Play can take place during focused teaching, where the practitioner works with a group of children to address a specific learning objective, and during independent activities, as summarized in Figure 1.1. In order for activities to be independent, they should be:

- freely chosen by the child

- interesting and motivating

- managed without the involvement of an adult

- open-ended.

Independent activities can fall into two categories:

(a) **Practitioner-initiated:** the practitioner suggests a mathematical task or idea for the children to pursue with a specific learning outcome in mind, which the children may address during their activity.

(b) **Child-initiated:** the youngsters might select resources available to them, plan their own activity and pursue their own learning agenda. Similarly, they may extend a practitioner-initiated activity to fit their own purpose.

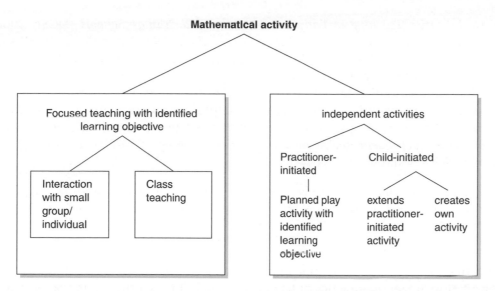

Figure 1.1   Mathematical activity

The provision of these equally valuable activities is in accordance with the *Statutory Framework for the Early Years Foundation Stage* which states that:

> All the areas must be delivered through planned, purposeful play, with a balance of adult-led and child-led activities. (DfES, 2007a: 11)

This is also very appropriate for children as they move into Key Stage 1.

Initially, however, most children will need some adult guidance to work independently, because they are immature and lack the requisite skills, or perhaps because they are more accustomed to sedentary 'holding' activities. In mixed year group classes, the role model of the older child in independent activities can be enormously beneficial. There are also several management issues to consider in order for independent activities to be successful:

- It must be made clear to the children which learning contexts are available – play trays, small world drama, role play, etc. (see Chapter 2).

- Independent activities should be 'advertised' clearly through a visual 'menu', or similar means (see Chapter 8).

- They should be introduced clearly, making planned learning objectives explicit through verbal prompts posed as questions or problems to be solved (see Examples in Chapters 4–7).

Once children have selected their activity, the practitioner must make time both to observe the independent work and to make quality interactions.

Transition

Transition from Foundation Stage to Key Stage 1 is a process, the success of which depends on the appropriate provision for each child. Both the *Independent Review of Mathematics Teaching in Early Years Settings and Primary Schools* (DCSF, 2008) and the *Independent Review of the Primary Curriculum: Final Report* (Rose, 2009) suggest that Year 1 teachers should consult the Early Years Foundation Stage Profile passed on to them by the Foundation teachers to inform them about the whole child as well as mathematical attainment. Abrupt changes in routines, teaching styles and learning environments are not helpful, particularly for those summer-born children who might only have experienced two terms in the Foundation Stage. The *Independent Review of Mathematics Teaching in Early Years Settings and Primary Schools* states:

> Familiar approaches to children's mathematical education should be maintained in Year 1, and Year 1 teachers should be encouraged to increase opportunities for active, independent learning and learning through play, as in the EYFS to ensure a continuation of positive attitudes to mathematics. (DCSF, 2008: 41)

Play, then, is endorsed as an appropriate context for mathematics teaching beyond Foundation Stage; the practice of teachers throughout the primary age range might be greatly informed by a study of early years mathematics pedagogy.

Play and the Primary National Strategy

The *Primary Framework for Literacy and Mathematics* (DfES, 2006) encourages teachers to be more flexible in their teaching. It sets out how its implementation will be characterized by making teaching 'vivid' and 'real'. Emphasizing the importance of play and making connections between aspects of learning, it encourages pedagogical choice and flexibility to ensure this happens. Mathematics lessons, and teaching sequences, if planned with playful and meaningful contexts in mind, can provide a continuum *between* 'work' and 'play' in the following ways:

- It is helpful to ensure mathematics occurs in a meaningful and stimulating context, such as linking it to the current theme or interests of the children. If the children are enjoying, say, *Mrs Mopple's Washing Line* (see Resources) in their literacy curriculum, then it must seem terribly disjointed for them to be counting cubes in maths, or measuring the length of their friend's arm, as demanded by their workbook. 'Helping' Mrs Mopple to solve some washing-related problem by counting pegs or measuring lengths of washing line puts the maths into a meaningful and less disjointed context.

- It makes good management sense for the practitioner, and creates meaningful links for the children, if learning contexts – play trays, role play, small worlds, etc. – are linked by a common theme through which different areas of the curriculum can be accessed (see Chapter 2). This can provide a meaningful learning context and encourage connection-making between experiences.

- It is worth varying the environment in which mathematics takes place, for example outside, inside or on the floor.

Four-year-olds entering school will not necessarily know if they are doing literacy, mathematics or science, but they will know if they are happily and meaningfully

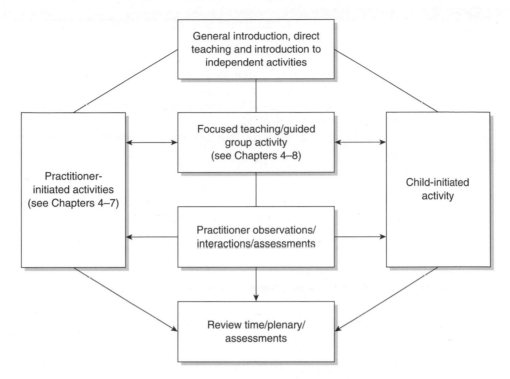

Figure 1.2   Model of an early years mathematics teaching session

occupied, and that their activity is valued by the practitioner. Figure 1.2 suggests a structure for a playful teaching session for single or mixed-age classes from Reception to Year 2.

It provides:

- a very short starter activity and class teaching time, in which all children are actively engaged, with the use of differentiated questioning

- the opportunity for all children, regardless of year group, to be involved in both their chosen independent activity and the focused teaching activity in the main part of the lesson. The practitioner works with identified groups of children, but also allows dedicated time for observations and interactions with children working independently. Focused teaching sessions and independent work happen concurrently

- a conclusion to the session with a review of work undertaken, involving revision of the learning objectives addressed through some developmentally appropriate activity like a song or 'maths story', and most importantly, the children are given time to report back on their independent learning. This is crucial in raising the profile of the activity and the self-esteem of the child, while providing further opportunities for practitioners to make formative assessments.

The ensuing chapters provide examples of teaching mathematics through play and playful context that are characteristic of effective early years pedagogy.

Creative ideas for good practice

- The provision of good quality play is vital for young children, enabling them to repeat, rehearse and refine a vast range of skills.
- Links should be made between areas of learning so that mathematics teaching is meaningful and makes sense to the child.
- Play must be well planned and resourced, highly valued and involve quality inter-actions with adults.
- Mathematics teaching should involve a balance of focused teaching and inde-pendent activities, both practitioner- and child-initiated.
- Practitioners should consider the ways in which they can embed play as a feature of effective early years mathematics pedagogy in their practice.

Suggested further reading

Athey, C. (1990) *Extending Thought in Young Children*: *A Parent–Teacher Partnership*. London: Paul Chapman Publishing.

Bennett, N., Wood, L. and Rogers, S. (1997) *Teaching Through Play: Teacher's Thinking and Classroom Practice*. Buckingham: Open University Press.

Craft, A. (2002) *Creativity in Early Years Education*. London: Continuum.

DCSF (2008) *Independent Review of Mathematics Teaching in Early Years Settings and Primary Schools*. London: DCSF.

Dowling, M. (2005) *Supporting Young Children's Sustained Shared Thinking: An Exploration*. London: Early Education.

Fisher, J. (2002) *Starting from the Child*. Buckingham: Open University Press.

Nutbrown, C. (1999) *Threads of Thinking*: *Young Children Learning and the Role of Early Education*, 2nd edition. London: Paul Chapman Publishing.

Pound, L. (1999) *Supporting Mathematical Development in the Early Years*. Buckingham: Open University Press.

Rogers, S. and Evans, J. (2008) *Inside Role-Play in Early Childhood Education*. London: Routledge.

Wood, E. and Atfield, J. (2005) *Play, Learning and the Early Childhood Curriculum*, 2nd edition. London: Paul Chapman Publishing.

2

Creating and using a mathematical environment

This chapter covers:

- the interplay between the psychological and the physical mathematical learning environment
- the features of an early years learning environment, and examples of how they can promote mathematical development and provide links with other areas of learning
- creative materials and resources
- creating and using mathematical displays
- mathematical activity in the outside environment.

Ethos

The environment plays a crucial role in a child's learning and consists of two main aspects: the psychological and the physical. No matter how well chosen the resources and how well planned the activities, if the children do not feel valued and secure, then they are unlikely to engage fully with the surroundings. In order for children to feel confident enough to make choices and take risks, the ethos needs to be one in which self-esteem is nurtured and independent learning encouraged. Interestingly, Worthington and Carruthers (2003) argue that the classrooms that support children's own mathematical graphics are the ones in which the psychological environment is of equal importance to the physical. The physical environment therefore needs to be planned in conjunction with management issues and pastoral care that foster independence and provide opportunities to acknowledge success.

The practical implications of this are as follows:

- Children must be given dedicated time and space to pursue a chosen activity.

- A sensitive balance must be ensured between focused teaching, practitioner-initiated activity and child-initiated activity, which can act to raise the profile of play and develop self-esteem and confidence in the child (see Chapter 1).

- The provision of dedicated time for children to talk about their activity and to promote sustained shared thinking through sensitive open questioning is crucial. Giving time for children to talk to one another, to practitioners and to a group or class collectively, emphasizes to the child the value placed upon the activity and, importantly, their interpretation and their involvement in it.

- It is important to display children's own recorded mathematics (see below), enabling the child to perceive themselves as a competent mathematician, thus raising their self-esteem.

The physical environment

Not only must the practitioner find ways to promote a positive ethos, but they must also create a physical environment rich in exciting opportunities for mathematical activity. Worthington and Carruthers (2003) suggest that if learning environments are mathematical, then mathematics happens. When planning the physical environment, consideration must be given to:

- appropriate resources to inspire and motivate children

- space to enable interaction with peers and a natural flow from one activity to the other

- time dedicated to exploring the opportunities they present.

Bilton (1998) argues that the place in which we expect learning to take place has to reflect the learning we expect. If we wish mathematical activity to occur, we must show evidence of it happening throughout the environment by examining every aspect of continuous provision for mathematical potential and communicating this to the learning community.

Selecting mathematical resources

Natural materials

While some commercial plastic resources do have their place, the majority have very limited possibilities. Good resources tend to be those that are aesthetic with potential for creative and cross-curricular opportunities such as natural objects. Conkers, acorns and shells, for example, provide excellent opportunities for counting in 1s, 2s, 5s, 10s, sorting and pattern making. Not only are these tactile, and therefore appealing to a young child, but they can provide meaningful links with other areas of learning:

- science (growth, materials)

- language (stimulating talk about similarities/differences, descriptive language)

- geography (places of origin, the local environment)

- history (will they always stay the same? What will happen if we plant them?)

- creative (using them for printing with, and as a stimulus for observational drawing and painting).

Such resources, offered in baskets or boxes, provide many opportunities for counting, weighing, sorting, capacity work and pattern making (see Chapters 4 and 5).

Numerals, number tracks and number lines

Children should have access to both number tracks (with numbered spaces representing natural counting numbers) and number lines (offering possibilities for representing numbers in between natural numbers). Numbers should be displayed for a variety of purposes, including reference during focused teaching.

Young children are often fascinated with big numbers and the provision of a number line to 100 around the room, preferably at child height, gives children excellent opportunities to see the development of the number system. Number lines or tracks can be presented as:

- a number snake or 'magic' path

- floor number lines big enough for the children to experience jumping forwards or back along the number line to explore the ordinal nature of number and mathematical operations in a physical way (see Chapter 4)

- empty number lines for children to annotate themselves and to encourage them to begin counting from a number other than 1, or to count in units of more than 1 (see Chapter 4).

Numerals should be seen in meaningful and purposeful contexts, for example on resources and on labels giving information such as '3 people can work in the graphics area'. It is useful to display the numeral along with the written word and an array (see Glossary) of the number to illustrate and reinforce the connection between the written word, symbol and array.

 Creative ideas for good practice

- Supply tactile numeral cards (made out of rough fabric, sandpaper, rope, etc.) and numeral marble runs.
- Provide areas in the environment where children can count interesting and aesthetic objects and label them with the corresponding numeral.
- Provide opportunities for children to see numerals alongside the written word and corresponding array.
- Display numerals in purposeful contexts (on drawers, pots of pencils, construction boxes, posters/signs, etc.).
- Ensure that number lines, both numbered and empty, are readily available for children to refer to and to write on independently.
- Display 'big' numbers, including a hundred square, prominently.
- Make number games readily available.
- Display books about number.

Other mathematical resources

Resources are most successful when they are theme-related and meaningful for the child, often being made simply and cheaply by both practitioners and children. This gives real meaning to the learning and a sense of ownership to the child (see Chapters 4–7). There are a few essential resources, however, that satisfy basic requirements:

- weighing apparatus – bucket balance, scales

- rulers and tape measures

- jugs and scoops of different sizes

- mathematical symbol cards/tiles

- construction kits, including sets of wooden blocks

- sets of 2D and 3D shapes

- calculators

- bead bars/strings

- counting sticks.

Use of space

In the early years learning environment, space should be designated for different areas of learning. The inside environment should provide a carpeted area, for sitting and working on the floor, and a small number of tables and chairs. A well-considered environment may allocate space for the following learning contexts:

- play trays

- small worlds

- role play

- a construction area

- a graphics area

- modelling/malleable materials

- a painting area

- a reading area

- a listening area

- a 'washing line'

- an ICT area.

Pound (1999: 31) suggests that mathematical contexts should 'reflect, explore and above all link with children's everyday experiences'. All of these contexts require careful planning in terms of resourcing and identified learning intentions (see Chapter 8) and can provide excellent, creative learning opportunities for young mathematicians (see Chapters 4–7).

Play trays

Traditionally known as sand and water trays, these trays have a far greater learning and creative potential than their original names might suggest. Depending on the contents of the tray, opportunities for counting, sorting, pattern making, mathematical operations, investigations into weight and length, and problem solving can be presented. By offering imaginative, independent play tray mathematical activities in a purposeful, story context, and by highlighting key questions and vocabulary, the practitioner can provide excellent learning contexts for the young mathematician. Possible play tray contents are:

- acorns

- buttons

- conkers

- cocoa pods

- corn

- cornflour and water ('gloop')

- dog biscuits

- fir/pine cones

- gravel

- leaves

- pasta (dried)

- paste (water and flour, coloured)

- porridge oats

- potting compost

- sawdust

- spaghetti (cooked, coloured, sprinkled in oil)

- straw

- twigs/bark

- wood shavings

- wood wool.

While the sturdier type of tray is more appropriate for denser, rougher materials, the small, round perspex trays are ideal for creating pond and other water-based mini-worlds. Some examples of mathematical play tray activities, and their links with other areas of the curriculum, are provided in Table 2.1.

Small world dramas

Small world dramas provide a specific type of role play that allows children to engage in imaginary play on a miniature scale. They can be presented on table-tops, the floor, or, indeed, in a play tray. Small worlds can be created by using the following resources:

- A selection of blue, green, brown and grey fabric/hessian to suggest the mini-world environment (fields, roads, seas, rivers, etc.).

- Plastic/wooden blocks placed beneath the fabric to create undulating landscapes.

- A selection of natural materials such as pine cones, small pieces of drift wood, bark, etc. to create shelters, enclosures, fencing and so on.

- Miniature animals, play people, houses/buildings and vehicles.

Owing to the 'bird's eye' view that children have of these mini-worlds, they offer excellent opportunities for the purposeful use of positional and spatial language, along with early geography skills (Rogers and Tucker, 2003; Tucker, 2002a; see also Chapter 6). Indeed, this can be developed by the inclusion of a bird, plane or hot-air balloon into the drama.

Role play

The provision of good quality role play is vital in any early years setting and provides young children with a creative context in which to practise and rehearse a wide range of skills. Typically, highly structured role play such as the café, vets' surgery and travel agents are often seen in early years classrooms. This often encourages the writing of lists, bills and receipts and the use of money to buy items and give change, all of which constitute mathematical play. This type of role play is particularly appropriate for older Key Stage 1 children who can practise associated mathematical skills stimulated by the theme and accompanying resources. Research (Rogers and Evans, 2008), however, suggests that the youngest children, aged three to five, benefit most from unstructured role-play using open-ended resources. This

Table 2.1 Mathematical play tray activities

Context for play and suggested resources	Concept/Skill	Examples of mathematical activity	Links with other areas of learning
Planting Potting compost; butter beans; plant pots (of different sizes); trowels	• estimating how many • counting • using vocabulary of number and capacity • exploring pouring and filling • comparing and ordering capacities	• filling and emptying plant pots • planting beans	• science – growth, materials • literacy – *Jasper's Beanstalk* by Nick Butterworth and Mick Inkpen
Dinosaur swamp Green paste (water, flour, green food colour); smooth twigs/driftwood; pebbles; plastic dinosaurs of different sizes	• ordering by size • counting • using vocabulary of number • partitioning	• lining up dinosaurs in order of size • constructing enclosures for the dinosaurs	• science – materials, changing materials • literacy – *Bumpus Jumpus Dinosaurumpus* by Tony Mitton and Guy Parker-Rees
In the wood Twigs; leaves; conkers; acorns; pieces of bark; plastic minibeasts	• making a sequence or pattern • counting • making fair shares	• lining up minibeasts in a sequence or pattern • making homes for equal numbers of minibeasts	• science – materials • geography – natural materials from local environment • literacy – *Ladybird, Ladybird* by Ruth Brown; *The Gruffalo* by Julia Donaldson and Axel Scheffler
Goldilocks Mugs of 'milk' for the three bears (water with a little white powder or liquid paint); 3 cups of different sizes; jugs	• exploring pouring and filling • estimating how much • comparing and ordering capacities	• filling and emptying cups of 'milk'	• science – changing materials • literacy – *Goldilocks and the Three Bears* (traditional)
Clothes Buttons of different shapes, colours and sizes; 'clothes', 'boots', 'shoes' (card outlines of trousers, dresses, boots, etc. covered in fabric)	• making a sequence or pattern • sorting • counting • using language of number • exploring and comparing areas	• selecting buttons to lie in a line on the front of the 'garment' • covering 'clothes' in buttons	• geography – clothes suitable for different weathers • art/design – selecting colour/style • literacy – *Jamaica and Brianna* by Juanita Havill and Anne Sibley O'Brien
Designing a garden Wet sand; dried/artificial flowers; pebbles; sticks; shells	• making a sequence or pattern • exploring properties of 2D shapes • using vocabulary of shape and position	• laying out pebbles, flowers, shells, etc. in a sequence or pattern • sculpting shapes	• science – materials • art – sculpture • literacy – *Mary, Mary Quite Contrary* (traditional); *The Sand Horse* by Ann Turnbull and Michael Foreman

(Continued)

Table 2.1 (Continued)

Context for play and suggested resources	Concept/Skill	Examples of mathematical activity	Links with other areas of learning
Jungle swamp 'Swamp' (green food colour in water); pebbles; drift wood/twigs; plastic snakes and lizards of different lengths	• comparing and ordering by length • counting • using language of number and measurement • making a sequence or pattern	• arranging creatures in order of length • laying out creatures in a sequence or pattern	• science – materials • geography – habitats • literacy – *The Enormous Crocodile* by Roald Dahl and Quentin Blake
On the farm Grain; small hessian sacks of different sizes; scoops	• exploring pouring and filling • estimating how many • counting • using language of number and capacity • comparing and ordering capacities	• filling and emptying sacks with grain	• science – materials, food • literacy – *Rosie's Walk* by Pat Hutchins
In the pet shop Dog biscuits (of different shapes and colours); thick paper bags; scoops	• sorting • making a sequence or pattern • counting • exploring properties of 2D shapes • exploring pouring and filling • estimating how many • using language of number and capacity	• selecting biscuits to put into bags • laying out biscuits in a sequence or pattern • filling and emptying bags	• science – food • literacy – *The Pet Shop* by Allan Ahlberg and Andre Amstutz; *A Bit More Bert* by Allan Ahlberg and Raymond Briggs
Noah's Ark 'Sea' (blue food colour in water); large plastic boat; twigs/drift wood; leaves/greenery; pairs of plastic animals; play people	• sorting • making a sequence/pattern • counting in 1s and 2s • partitioning	• matching animals • laying out animals in a sequence or pattern • marching animals into the ark	• literacy/KE – *Noah's Ark* (traditional) • science – materials
Fishing game Numbered laminated card fish with paper-clip attachments; fishing rods (dowelling, string with magnet)	• counting • numeral recognition • addition by counting on	• counting fish caught • reading numeral on fish • devising simple games	• science – magnets • literacy – *The Mousehole Cat* by Antonia Barber and Nicola Bayley
Animal journey Cocoa pods; 'lake' (card covered in silver paper); stones; twigs; greenery; plastic animals (mice, frogs, butterflies, lizards, crickets, etc.); play people	• sorting • counting • making a sequence or pattern • partitioning • making fair shares	• putting animals into like groups • laying out animals in a sequence or pattern • making enclosures for animals	• science – materials • geography – habitats, Africa • literacy – *Handa's Hen* and *Handa's Surprise* by Eileen Browne

Photo 2.1   The 'instant' flower shop role play provides opportunities for using money that the current role play area does not.

approach provides young children with more opportunities to negotiate and apply emerging social skills and enables them to fulfil their strong sense to self-generate play themes. This is both crucial for the child and informative for the practitioner; it provides a window through which the practitioner can see the child 'being' and where the child needs to go next. Focused observations and discussions with the child about their play give practitioners a valuable insight into the child's mathematical world. Observations may reveal whether the children are:

- using mathematical vocabulary with understanding

- showing signs of particular mathematical schemas

- displaying understanding of basic mathematical concepts

- showing new interests, on which future focused teaching sessions and continuous provision might be based.

Practitioners, then, should consider very carefully the provision of highly structured role play for the youngest children. Structured role play, appropriate for older children, is typically provided in a designated area, either inside or outside, but it can also be 'instant' role play (Burke et al., 2002; Tucker, 2002a). By dedicating a table and accompanying basket of suitable props, a shop, ticket office, fruit stall, etc. can be established quickly and effectively. This is particularly useful for those practitioners who work in limited space or for those whose children are currently enjoying play in a role-play area whose theme does not have realistic links with money, for example.

Table 2.2 suggests mathematical activities provided by some popular early years themes while the list below suggests resources to stimulate mathematical opportunities. Open-ended resources might include:

- plain tabards

- scarves/lengths of fabric

- large wooden blocks/crates/wooden frames for den making

- cardboard tubes and boxes of varying sizes

- writing materials

- counting collections (see Chapter 4)

- 'treasure' (old jewellery/glass beads)

- bunches of keys

- bowls, plates, cups, tankards in different materials.

The following resources provide mathematical opportunities in structured role play:

- address books

- appointment books/cards

- a bucket balance

- calendars

- calculator

- a cash till

- cheque books

- clocks (digital and analogue with clear numerals)

- coins

- credit cards

- dials (real or made by the practitioner or children)

- diaries/log books

- dressing-up clothes of different sizes

- forms (both real and made by the practitioner and children)

Table 2.2 Mathematical opportunities in role play

Concept/Skill	Possible mathematical activities in the Flower Shop	Possible mathematical activities in the Health Centre	Possible mathematical activities in the Pirates' Voyage
Reading/Writing numerals	• using cash till/telephone/ calendar/credit cards • making price tags • filling in order forms • writing addresses and telephone numbers • writing cheques • writing opening/closing times • labelling displays	• writing/reading appointment cards • using calendar/telephone • writing in/reading appointment book • writing prescriptions • writing addresses • using waiting number tags	• reading numerals on doubloons • recording times/dates/items of treasure found in log book • using/making maps
Counting	• flowers in 1s, 2s, 5s, 10s • message cards in packs of 10 • rolls of ribbons • number of plant pots	• number of patients • appointment cards in 1s, 2s, 5s, 10s • prescription bundles	• counting biscuits/rations • treasure • doubloons in 1s and bags of 10s
Ordering	• items on the shelf in price order • plant pots by size • flowers by stem length	• patients in the queue • position in queue number tags	• telescopes by length • bags of treasure by weight
Sorting	• ribbon by colour/length • flowers by colour • plant pots by size • flowers by stem length • coins in cash till	• bandages, plasters, medicine bottles	• jewels/treasure/doubloons
Mathematical operations	• calculating prices • giving change • calculating total number of flowers/message cards by counting in 2s, 5s, 10s	• calculating total number of appointment cards by counting in 10s	• sharing jewels/doubloons among the crew • finding total amount of doubloons
Pattern	• flowers by colour for window display • pots and flowers for display		• hanging small coloured flags (bunting) in a pattern

(Continued)

Table 2.2 (Continued)

Concept/Skill	Possible mathematical activities in the Flower Shop	Possible mathematical activities in the Health Centre	Possible mathematical activities in the Pirates' Voyage
Weighing	• amount of flower bulbs		• estimating/comparing weight of treasure
Measuring length	• estimating/measuring length of ribbon • estimating/measuring length of flower stems	• estimating/measuring length of bandages	• estimating/measuring lengths of telescopes/bunting
Time	• using clock • making/displaying opening and closing time signs • recording times of deliveries	• using clock • giving appointment times • displaying opening/closing times • measuring time for each patient	• recording dates in log book
Shape and space	• wrapping flowers in differently shaped paper/cellophane	• applying bandages	• making small flags • drawing picture maps
Capacity	• filling paper bags with flower bulbs	• filling boxes with rolls of bandages	• filling bags/boxes with treasure
Using money	• making amounts • giving change		• using doubloons as currency

- jugs/containers (of different sizes)

- numeral cards (for numbering patients' beds in the hospital etc.)

- price tags

- recipes

- stamps

- tape measures

- telephones

- a telephone directory

- writing materials, including squared paper (for shopping lists, telephone numbers and messages).

The graphics area

This is a dedicated 'work station' for writing, drawing, booklet and label making. It provides an ideal area for combining literacy and mathematical graphics. In order to stimulate and motivate mathematical activity here, consider providing the following resources:

- paper of varying colour, shapes and sizes (including squared paper)

- pencils and coloured pens

- scissors

- glue sticks

- a stapler

- sellotape

- ready-made booklets of differing sizes

- number lines (including empty number lines)

- sheets of large numerals (suitable for cutting out)

- sheets of mathematical vocabulary (suitable for cutting out)

- plastic 2D shapes (for drawing around)

- a ruler.

Practitioner- and child-initiated activities might include:

- making booklets about shapes found in the learning environment, long and short things, things of a specific length, things heavier/lighter than a theme-related object, favourite numbers, patterns, telephone numbers

- making price tags for a shop

- making numbered tickets

- designing/making order forms

- making posters depicting numerals

- making birthday cards.

The construction area

In her study into block play, Gura (1992) describes in detail how manipulating and building with bricks supports mathematical development in terms of opportunities to explore individual shapes and the spatial relationship between them, developing strategies for using the blocks to record their mathematical thinking and to encourage problem solving. When supplying construction equipment, it is useful to consider the following points:

- Provide a mix of wooden blocks (because of their simplicity and aesthetic nature) and commercial kits (more prescriptive in terms of possibilities, but designed for young children to fit together for a purpose).

- Label construction boxes clearly with a picture of the contents and the number of pieces held within. Not only does it facilitate order when tidying away, but it gives real purpose to sorting and counting, emphasizing the relationship between ordinal and cardinal numbers (see Glossary).

- Provide 'Can you ...?' cards. After initial exploration of a kit, these present a task related to the theme and interest of the children where the practitioner can highlight a specific mathematical concept, such as 'Can you make a model with 6 wheels?', or 'Can you make a box long enough for the snake?' (with a toy snake for the child to use in the comparison of length). Writing materials can be provided for children to record their responses.

Reading and listening areas

The reading area, like the graphics area, provides another ideal space for promoting links between literacy and mathematics. There are many excellent and engaging storybooks available that use a mathematical concept as their theme (see Resources). Storybooks that have measurement as a theme, for example, can be displayed prominently alongside a poster depicting relevant mathematical vocabulary, and resources the children have used in measuring. This enables the children to make connections between their own experience, and that depicted by characters in the book.

Similarly, audio books can be made available in the listening corner, along with CDs of number rhymes and songs. It is also valuable to give the children the opportunity to make up their own number rhymes, which they can record and share with their peers in this area.

Malleable materials and the painting area

Modelling dough and clay should be available for exploration and these materials can also be used to support mathematical development. Modelling dough can be used to:

- sculpt numerals

- make theme-related objects or characters of differing length and width, which the children can compare and measure

- make 3D shapes, providing excellent opportunities to explore ways in which shapes can be studied through stretching and compression

- explore numbers in conjunction with theme-related objects, for example putting the corresponding number of pennies into modelling dough numerals, or exploring the 'fourness of four' by incorporating four conkers, four twigs, four shells, etc. into a theme-related dough or clay model.

Paint can be used in a variety of ways to develop further mathematical skills and concepts. Ways of using paint might include:

- using it as another medium for recording mathematical graphics

- creating patterns

- mark-making to stimulate mathematical vocabulary relating to shape, space and position.

ICT

This area often has a computer, programmable toy (see Chapter 6), CD player and recording equipment. The recording equipment can be used to play simple games, such as picking a numeral card at random and recording the corresponding number of claps. Children can also record their own number rhymes, or practise and record counting in 2s, 5s and 10s. They can then play this back to a friend who can work out what unit they are counting in.

Programmable toys can be used to explore mathematical concepts in conjunction with a small world layout on the floor (see Chapter 6).

The washing line

As its name suggests, this is literally a piece of washing line, suspended at child height, across the length of a wall or corner of the room. Where the layout of the indoor learning space does not allow for either of these, it can be attached to two cones and brought out when needed. It is ideal for sequencing numerals and measures (including big pictures of coins) or constructing patterns along its length.

Photo 2.2   A child displaying his independent mathematical graphics.

Displays

All too often, maths displays are merely the record of work undertaken in focused teaching – the final product that requires no further involvement, and to all intents and purposes can be ignored (Tucker, 2001a). It is important to display a balance of recorded work: work that is practitioner-led, practitioner-initiated and child-initiated. Displays depicting mathematics recorded in child-initiated activity are rarely a feature of early years classrooms (Worthington and Carruthers, 2003) and is a sad reflection of the status it has. Often, children's own mathematical work is not aesthetically pleasing and might be difficult to interpret, but this is no reason to avoid displaying it. With helpful comments from the practitioner displayed alongside, this work can be interpreted by all.

 Principles into practice

- Provide a display board at child height specifically for children's independent mathematical graphics. This allows children to select and display their own work, thus giving them ownership of the process.
- Allow children to 'publish' their own booklets about mathematical concepts and display these alongside real books about the same maths theme.
- Where the nature of the recorded work is not immediately accessible to others, display explanations of the intended communication alongside.

Good mathematics displays need to be interactive and can be a mix of 2D and 3D displays that change each day, provide information about certain routines, and which the children can manipulate. They take a variety of forms:

- data displaying the contents of the snack basket or lunch preferences

- wall displays involving counting or pattern that can be discussed and changed daily. This stimulates lots of real mathematical talk and encourages the children to look out for pattern when they come into the learning environment in the morning (see Chapter 5)

- 3D displays of objects for children to manipulate, count, order by specific criteria or arrange in a pattern (see Chapter 4)

- photographs of mathematical activities in role-play situations, or the outside environment, accompanied by written descriptions, or documentation

- themed displays showing connections between mathematics and other areas of learning.

 Creative ideas for good practice

- Provide laminated square pieces of card depicting the snack or type of lunch so that the children can make their own recording in the form of a pictogram (see Glossary), giving them ownership of the display and providing them with real and useful information. The same information can be presented in 3D form by the children making a column of bricks, each of which depicts the information it represents.
- Use children's theme-related paintings for pattern making, such as different sized leaves on a giant beanstalk, garments on a washing line, or toy vehicles in a traffic jam.
- During a theme about the garden centre, for example, display baskets of large seeds, small plastic wallets, and mathematical questions alongside. By counting and bagging the seeds in 10s, a quick and effective display can be made to show what 100 actually looks like.
- Put numerals on made and displayed objects from other areas of learning, such as on cardboard lighthouses made during technology. Once displayed on blue fabric with stones and boats, it will stimulate small world play in which the children can take the boats on journeys, visiting the lighthouses in numerical order.

Display checklist

- Are the children involved in making the display?
- If the display is of completed work, what questions need to be displayed alongside to encourage reflection and talk?
- What information/types of questions need to be displayed to enable parents/carers and others to understand and value the child's work?
- Are all aspects of mathematics displayed over the course of a term?
- What resources or questions could be added to displays from other curriculum areas to help create a mathematical learning environment?

Photo 2.3   Including numerals and simple artefacts in this technology display stimulates small world play with a mathematical content.

The outside environment

The learning contexts and resources detailed above are by no means exclusive to the inside environment and, without exception, they can be offered outdoors. There is huge potential for teaching and learning across the curriculum in the outside environment (Bilton, 1998; Ouvry, 2003; Rhydderch-Evans, 1993). This section will consider how the dedicated outside play area may be used to promote play in mathematical development.

In order to unify good quality provision within the indoor and outdoor learning environments, the practitioner might consider the following points:

- ensuring continuity of management strategies and ethos between inside and outside

- giving equal status to the teaching and learning of mathematics in each environment

- planning to ensure meaningful links between inside and outside themes and learning areas

- planning for equal opportunity (including ensuring all year groups have access to the outdoors in a mixed year group class)

- providing quality and appropriate resources

- providing dedicated time and space for mathematical activity

- allowing free-flow access between the environments where this is physically possible, and where it is not, ensuring that children have good 'chunks' of the day outside

- planning, assessing and evaluating mathematics inside and outside.

 Principles into practice

During a theme on 'clothes', practitioners might plan:

- launderette role play inside, while outside there may be washing lines, streets of clothes shops built out of blocks, ride-on 'delivery vans' delivering 'dry-cleaning', numbered parking spaces, etc.
- that all practitioners working in the team spend time in both environments, ensuring that children do not perceive practitioners as 'the inside one' or 'the outside one'
- that a balance of focused teaching and independent activity is carried out and assessed in each environment
- to display photographs of mathematical activities and recorded work from both environments.

In terms of outside provision, Bilton (1998: 40) suggests the following learning areas, or bays:

- an imaginative area

- a building and construction area

- a gymnasium area

- a small apparatus area

- a horticultural area

- an environmental and scientific area

- a quiet area.

In addition to this, a graphics area could be provided, offering the resources and opportunities previously described. This might consist of a box or trolley containing the resources and a stool and writing table constructed with hollow blocks. Table 2.3 suggests how these learning bays might be presented to support mathematical development.

Resources that support outdoor mathematical development include:

- big number tiles, digit cards and numbered cones

- cones numbered in multiples of 10s – this is particularly useful if the children are engaged in counting large numbers of interesting leaves or stones that they have collected

Table 2.3   Mathematical opportunities outside

Learning bay	Features stimulating mathematical activity
Imaginative	(In addition to role-play resources list) • dressing-up clothes on numbered hangers • signposts • road signs
Building and construction	• numbered and labelled construction kits/trolleys • wooden planks/bamboo/tubing/guttering of different lengths and widths • diggers/ride-on toys with number plates • road signs illustrating speeds, distances • frames to encourage tessellating unit blocks, such as plywood 'roof' with rim
Gymnasium	• numbered ladders and A-frames • equipment laid out in identifiable sequence or pattern, straight or curved lines • tunnels of different lengths
Small apparatus	• equipment stored in bags of 2s, 5s, 10s • numbered cones • access to games/targets that encourage numeral recognition/ shape recognition/counting • sand timers to mark start/stop for specific games
Horticultural	• laminated labels indicating dates of planting/order of planting – 1st, 2nd, 3rd • equipment, including clipboard, for measurement and recording • tubs/flower pots of graduated size
Environmental and scientific	• buckets/watering cans of different capacities • funnels of graduated size • laminated questions such as, 'How many ladybirds can you find today?' • play tray activities • selection of natural materials presented in such a way as to encourage pattern making
Quiet area	• number mat • books depicting number and mathematical skills and concepts (see Resources) • mathematical rhymes and story tapes

- permanent ground markings, such as parking spaces, number lines, number snakes and decision trees. If these are left unnumbered, the children can number them themselves using number cones or tiles

- containers that can be labelled and numbered to provide further opportunities for sorting, counting and numeral recognition. These also create links with inside management (Bilton, 1998).

Undoubtedly, the provision of quality outdoor mathematical activities offers children a creative and intellectual freedom the inside environment does not (Bilton, 1998; Ouvry, 2003). Bilton (1998) argues that if the more formal curriculum is brought outside into this freer, less pressurized atmosphere and presented as play, some children, particularly boys, can access it more easily, using the knowledge they gain from the activity in the inside environment later on. Practitioners should therefore strive to plan mathematical opportunities outside, not least because it facilitates more appropriate modes of learning. Table 2.4 illustrates how natural links between the inside and outside environments can be used effectively in the teaching and learning of mathematics in mixed Foundation Stage and Key Stage 1 classes. It illustrates mathematical opportunities based on the theme of 'Sukkot', the Jewish autumn festival (see Glossary).

Table 2.4 Mathematical activities for Sukkot

Activity	Environment	Opportunities for mathematics
Cooking biscuits for 'celebratory' meal. Counting 10 biscuits on each plate	Inside	• weighing ingredients • counting in 1s and groups of 10s • measuring capacity • using related mathematics vocabulary
Collecting natural materials (branches, ivy, leaves) for roof construction	Outside	• discussion of shapes and sizes of leaves • comparison of lengths of leaves and branches • discussion of patterns on leaves • use of mathematical vocabulary
Construction of three-sided structure for sukkah using hollow wooden blocks/crates	Outside	• discussion of optimum size and position • exploration of tessellation of blocks and shapes' properties • measurement of height, depth, width • exploration of symmetry • problem solving – will it be big enough for us?
Decorating sukkah by constructing paper chains and making celebratory posters	Outside or Inside	• constructing paper chains in colour pattern, such as blue, red, blue, red • incorporating 2D shapes and numerals into posters
Pouring drinks for celebratory meal	Inside or outside	• using mathematical vocabulary of volume and capacity • measuring capacity • counting • equal shares
Developing role play using celebratory meal and previous discussions about Sukkot as stimulus	Outside	• sharing biscuits and drinks fairly • 'reading' mathematical posters • addressing/reading invitations to celebratory meal • counting/setting places for celebratory meal

Creative ideas for good practice

• Encourage a positive ethos in the learning environment which enables children to perceive themselves as competent and enthusiastic mathematicians.
• Provide interactive displays, labels and signs that support mathematical thinking and activity.

(Continued)

(Continued)

- Establish creative, well-planned contexts for play which promote the use of mathematical vocabulary and for which there are clearly identified learning intentions.
- Ensure all areas of the learning environment provide rich mathematical opportunities in order to facilitate good quality child-initiated mathematical learning.
- Provide dedicated time and space for children to use the learning environment for both practitioner-initiated and child-initiated play, and use the environment to show how these are valued.
- Give equal status to the teaching and learning of mathematics in both outside and inside environments.

Suggested further reading

Bilton, H. (2004) *Playing Outside: Activities, Ideas and Inspiration for the Early Years*. London: David Fulton Publishers.

Carruthers, E. and Worthington, M. (2006) *Making Marks, Making Meaning*, 2nd edition. London: Sage Publications.

Drake, J. (2003) *Organising Play in the Early Years*. London: David Fulton Publishers.

Fisher, J. (2002) *Starting from the Child*. Buckingham: Open University Press.

Howe, A. (2005) *Play Using Natural Materials*. London: David Fulton Publishers.

Pond, L. (2008) *Thinking and Learning about Mathematics in the Early Years*. London: Routledge.

Thornton, L. and Brunton, P. (2005) *Understanding the Reggio Approach*. London: David Fulton Publishers.

3

Creative recording and mathematical graphics

This chapter covers:

- a discussion of the limitations of recording mathematics on worksheets
- the meaning of mathematical graphics
- ways to stimulate and support mathematical graphics through play
- examples of mathematical graphics stimulated by play from Foundation Stage to Year 2.

The worksheet or creative recording?

Traditionally, the worksheet has ruled when it comes to recording mathematics, be it in the form of colouring in, or the filling in of empty boxes. While some schools and early years settings rely heavily on worksheets, anecdotal evidence suggests that many practitioners and teachers are becoming more willing to encourage children to record their mathematics on whiteboards, while others use a mix of both whiteboards and worksheets. The continued popularity of worksheets seems to be two-fold; they are an easy option for the practitioner (no preparation required, sedentary children and no cleaning up afterwards) and they generate easily accessible responses. Meanwhile, shelves of revision guides and workbooks in bookshops suggest to parents that the use of worksheets brings success. By their very nature, workbooks and sheets, often being curricular and objective driven, cannot begin with what individual children know, or indeed what interests them. They rarely inspire creativity, they do not offer opportunities for the children to make meaningful links between aspects of their learning and they do not promote sustained shared thinking. Indeed, the EYFS (DfES, 2007b) comments: 'it is difficult for children to make creative connections in their learning when colouring a worksheet' (4.3). The worksheet demands that every child should respond in the same way using the same format. Not only will the worksheet inhibit creativity but will often introduce young children to formal mathematical symbols in a decontextualized manner too early which, crucially, can be detrimental to later mathematical development (Pound, 1999).

The EYFS and the PNS fully support children's own mathematical mark-making, suggesting practitioners should value children's own mathematical graphic and practical explorations. Indeed, the *Independent Review of Mathematics Teaching in Early Years Settings and Primary Schools* (DCSF, 2008) states:

> Early years practitioners should encourage mathematical mark-making and open-ended discussion (or sustained shared thinking) in children's mathematical development. (2008: 34)

The Review describes how practitioners should work to establish a 'culture with significant focus on mathematical mark-making' (p. 37) in an environment where children can choose to use their own mathematical graphics to support their mathematical thinking. However, practitioners lack real guidance in supporting children's own mathematical recording as there are no examples provided in any of the legislated documentation. While many early years practitioners feel confident with emergent writing, few feel so with regard to 'emergent mathematics'. Consequently, many practitioners remain unsure how to support this creative approach. This lack of clear guidance has led many practitioners to introduce formal standard methods too soon or ignore children's own written methods (Carruthers and Worthington, 2006).

What are mathematical graphics?

Mathematical graphics are the tool of the developing or 'emerging' mathematician. The notion of 'emergent maths' is not at all new. Much has been written about the emergent approach; ideas have been brought together by Sue Atkinson (1992) who espoused the idea of children's apprenticeship approach to mathematics, developing maths in a meaningful context with children exploring their own ways of recording. Mathematical graphics, then, are inventive notations or physical arrangements freely chosen and created by the child in a meaningful context to represent mathematical thought. Such arrangements might be constructed out of bricks, pine cones, assorted objects or with paint, chalk and pen. In their extensive research into mathematical graphics, Carruthers and Worthington (2006) suggest that children move from gesture, movement and speech to their own exploration with marks and that they need to represent quantities that are counted before they progress to recording mathematical operations (where counting is continuous). Indeed, they suggest a development of 'dimensions' from ages three to eight:

- multi-modal explorations and explorations with marks

- early written numerals

- numerals as labels

- a representation of quantities and counting

- early operations: development of children's own written methods. (2006: 91)

Children will not, however, move systematically through the dimensions; some children may work within one dimension significantly longer than another, while others might appear to miss out a dimension and move on rapidly. The dimensions do, however, provide a window into understanding how mathematical graphics begin and how they might best be supported in settings and classrooms where the EYFS and the PNS are already embedded in daily practice. The development and examples that follow, based on the dimensions of Carruthers and Worthington (2006), illustrate how independently constructed mathematical graphics might be supported, observed and assessed for children up to and including Year 2.

Development and examples

Explorations with marks

Young children's mark-making may involve repeated behaviours such as the manipulation and arrangement of everyday objects, and scribbling with pens, chalk, and other writing media. Athey (1990) describes these repeated patterns of behaviour as 'schemas' and suggests that they often suggest mathematical thought and investigation. Through these repeated behaviours such as pouring and filling or laying objects in straight lines, children are making discoveries about capacity, volume, shape, length, perimeter and repeating pattern (see Chapter 9). As well as making marks by using physical objects in arrangements, young children are often seen 'scribbling' with pens or paint. On closer observation, these scribbles often hold significant meaning for the child. Only on discussion with the child and an understanding of the context in which the marks are made, are their mathematical significance revealed.

 Freya's number line

Context: Nursery

Freya, along with a small group of children spontaneously began to play with a large, roll-out number line from 0 to 10. They laid it out and took it in turns to jump along, counting jumps as they did so. They repeated this for several minutes and as the play began to break down, their practitioner suggested that they might like to make their own number line. With activity now refocused, the children collected paper and pens and, working on the floor, began to write their own number line. Freya worked silently at her number line for about 15 minutes (Figure 3.1).

Teacher's notes on discussion with the child:

- Freya described the top line as 'numbers'. She demonstrated that she understands the idea of a number line as a continuous line of numerals as labels and which here represent counting.
- The next two lines are repeating patterns. 'H, F, H, F' represents 'Holly, Freya, Holly, Freya' followed by a 'big dot, little dot' pattern. She shows a sound understanding of simple, repeating pattern and she is beginning to make links between patterns and the number line.
- The last line is a '4 number line'. Freya is 4 years old and therefore this number is significant to her.

(Continued)

(Continued)

- Freya's last line is a 'beach number line with shells and sea'. As her number line develops, she continues to make connections with other experiences involving lines, counting and patterns.

Next steps:

- Ensure that Freya has plenty of opportunities to use and make a variety of number lines as they have clearly captured her interest.
- Support the understanding of the connections Freya is beginning to make between pattern and the number line, for example by matching Numicon plates (see Chapter 4) to numeral along the number line. This will also allow her to see the connections between the ordinal and cardinal aspects of number.

Figure 3.1   Freya's number line

Early written numerals

Children's early mathematical graphics may reflect a mix of letters and numerals, as seen in Freya's number line (Figure 3.1). Occasionally, they may use their own numeral system where they ascribe a number to the same mark consistently over a period of time. Similarly, they may make significant marks to which they later ascribe a numeral.

Numerals as labels

Once children have experienced writing numerals as an integral part of their play, such as in their role play, and have become more confident with their use, they may then begin to use numerals as labels. Their drawings might, for example, show a birthday cake with a '3' on it, thus illustrating a numeral that is personal to them. This gives us a window into how they are making sense of their world and the connections they are making between what they observe and what they do.

 ### Charlotte's houses

Context: Reception class

Following discussion about houses and subsequent domestic role play, Charlotte went to the graphics area. Her teacher had provided some house-shaped zigzag books that day and Charlotte began creating her 'street' (Figure 3.2).

Figure 3.2   Charlotte's houses

Teacher's notes on discussion with the child:

- Charlotte's own house is number 11 and so she decided she would write this on one of her houses. She described 4 as her 'favourite number' and decided she would put it on the last house 'because I like 4'.

(Continued)

(Continued)

- Charlotte can write and recognize 11 and 4.
- Charlotte understands that numerals seen in the environment have significance and that she is beginning to understand the broad function of numbers.
- Charlotte understands that numbers of personal significance can be committed to paper as a numerical label.

Next steps:

- Give Charlotte a range of opportunities to write numerals and to notice when her graphics reflect an understanding of the ordinal nature of number.

Representations of quantities and counting

Young children are often fascinated by big numbers, revelling in the thought that a number can not only exceed their own age, but that they can go on and on. While they may yet be unable to write numerals that accurately represent either a counted large quantity, or an estimate of one, they can confidently make marks to represent their thoughts of the 'bigness' of numbers.

 Dillon's pancakes

Context: Nursery class in a primary school

On Shrove Tuesday, Dillon had listened to *The Story of Little Babaji* by Helen Bannerman (see Resources) and was interested in the large number of pancakes made and eaten at the end of the story. Dillon joined a group of children who were role playing making and eating pancakes. He spontaneously collected some circular paper from the graphics area and drew circle shapes all over it (Figure 3.3).

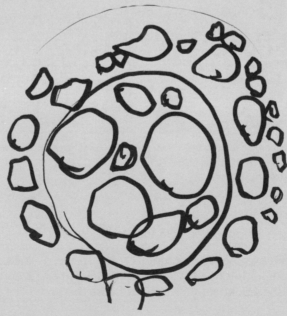

Figure 3.3   Dillon's pancakes

Teacher's notes on discussion with the child:

- Dillon described how his marks showed all the pancakes that were made in his role play. He began to count each circle, counting accurately until he reached 28 and then he said 'lots and lots of pancakes'.
- Dillon was clearly captivated by the thought of making and eating over 100 pancakes, as described in the book.
- Dillon was eager to represent a large number, and although he was unable to write a corresponding numeral, he was confident enough to make marks, which expressed his mathematical thoughts.

Next steps:

- Provide opportunities for counting large quantities and write corresponding numerals both in focused teaching groups and when it arises naturally.
- Encourage Dillon to see numerals representing large quantities in the learning environment and ensure he has opportunities to write them.

Mathematical operations

As children record a calculation, their graphics might include a mix of drawings, numerals, number lines and standard symbols. Often, the drawings will be pertinent to the 'maths story', that is the context in which the calculation is set. It is helpful to refer to these drawings as 'maths drawings', helping the child to differentiate between the purpose of quick, meaningful marks used to support mathematical calculation and a drawing in art. As the child becomes more confident and competent, they will gradually reduce non-standard marks and place greater emphasis on standard symbols.

 ### Isabella's farm

Context: Reception class

Isabella was involved in farm small world play. Her teacher had prepared a table with a variety of small world objects (see Chapters 2 and 4) to enable the children to make enclosures for farm animals and develop a related narrative. She had left a clipboard and paper nearby for children to record their mathematical responses to her challenge: 'The farmer needs some pens built for the animals. Can you put some animals into the pens and make a record of what you have done for the farmer?' (Figure 3.4).

Teacher's notes on discussion with the child:

- Referring to her written record at review time, Isabella described how she had made 2 fields with pine cones and had put 2 cows in one field and 3 cows in the other. She counted 5 cows all together and pointed to the numerals correctly.
- Isabella is able to use 'maths drawings' to support her thinking.
- Isabella shows a clear understanding of addition as the union of two sets.

(Continued)

(Continued)

Figure 3.4   Isabella's farm

- As Isabella reads through her emergent algorithm, she implies an understanding of a '+' sign although it is not written.
- Isabella shows an increased understanding of the = sign.

Next steps:

- Provide opportunities for Isabella to see the use of standard signs modelled in a variety of situations, both in daily routines and in focused teaching sessions, reinforcing their name and meaning.
- Encourage further use in playful contexts followed by discussion to clarify any misconceptions.

 Thomas' frogs

Context: Year 1 class

Thomas played with a play tray set up as a pond in his Year 1 classroom (see Chapter 4). His teacher had suggested that he re-enact a song about five speckled frogs in which, one by one, the frogs jump into the pond, and that he could write the corresponding algorithms on a clipboard nearby (Figure 3.5).

Teacher's notes on discussion with the child:

- Thomas was able to read through his list of algorithms accurately, explaining that once all 5 frogs had jumped in, there were none left, which was represented by 0. He explained he had started to write a number line and make a 'maths drawing', but hadn't continued. He explained that the drawing he made shows the first frog jumping into the pond.

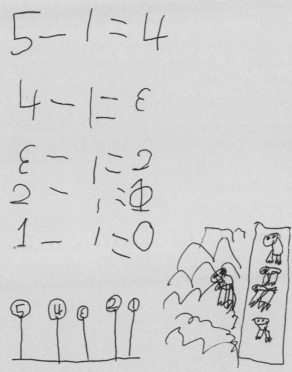

Figure 3.5   Thomas' frogs

- Thomas has a sound grasp of subtraction as take away.
- Thomas' recorded work shows his ability to self-correct. He was able to recognize that $2 - 1 = 0$ is not correct and was able to correct it accordingly.
- Thomas is moving away from a dependence on 'maths drawings' and is confidently using standard notation here.

Next steps:

- Encourage Thomas to look for patterns in similar calculations.

 ## The bakery

Context: Year 2

The children had been involved in 'bakery' maths as a playful context in which to explore multiplication as repeated addition. The teacher posed a 'special offer' problem for a group of children: 'Each customer coming into the shop today gets 3 free cupcakes. Talk about and show how you could calculate how many cupcakes the bakery will need to provide.' Three children worked together on shared graphics (Figure 3.6).

Teacher's notes on discussion with the children:

- The children worked methodically calculating the number of cakes for up to 6 customers and their recorded work showed a mix of 'maths drawings' and standard algorithms. They were able to explain their thinking and choice of standard symbols.

(Continued)

(Continued)

- Their drawings and addition algorithms accurately reflected their thinking, although they show some misunderstanding when recording multiplication algorithms.

Next steps:

- Reinforce correct recording of multiplication algorithms and ensure children understand how, for example, 3 + 3 + 3 + 3 is 3 × 4.

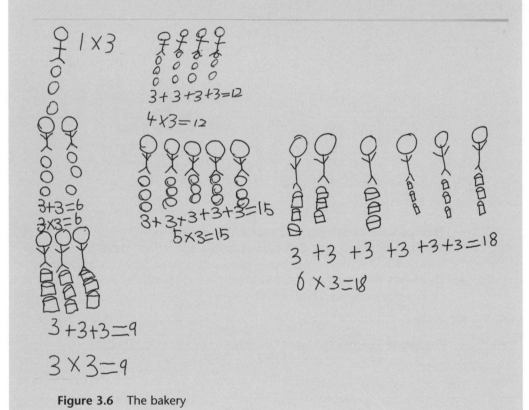

Figure 3.6   The bakery

Principles into practice

- Avoid opening focused teaching sessions by writing an example of a mathematical recording. This is likely to become copied by the children and therefore will not reflect their true thinking and understanding.
- Before the children make any mathematical marks, encourage them to talk about what they might draw or write to help them, both with the adult and with their peers.

- Model algorithms during the session when it is appropriate, after observing the children's recorded work and some assessment of their understanding has been made.
- Give the children time to talk about their mathematical recording both to one another and to the group.
- Give opportunities for children to talk about which type of graphics they found the most useful and why.

Getting started

If teachers and practitioners are currently using traditional methods for recording mathematics such as workbooks and sheets, moving wholesale to a culture of mathematical graphics will undoubtedly seem overwhelming. Ensuring that children have opportunities to create their own mathematical graphics and, most importantly, have many opportunities to see others, both adults and children, make mathematical graphics and talk about them is crucial. Table 3.1 gives some exemplars of how teachers

Table 3.1 Opportunities for modelling written calculations in daily routines

Opportunity	Exemplar
Number songs	Five currant buns Write algorithm $5 - 1 = 4$ $4 - 1 = 3$ $3 - 1 = 2$ $2 - 1 = 1$ $1 - 1 = 0$ as each bun is bought.
Discussion of lunch numbers	'There are 29 people here today. 20 people are having a school dinner. How many are having a packed lunch?' $29 - 20 = 9$
Planting seeds	There are 6 people in the group. Each person will plant 3 seeds. How many seeds will we need? $3 + 3 + 3 + 3 + 3 + 3 = 18$ $3 \times 6 = 18$
Giving out clipboards	There are 12 clipboards and 4 groups. How many clipboards will each group have? $12 \div 4 = 3$
Stacking chairs	The chairs are in 5 groups of 4. $4 + 4 + 4 + 4 + 4 = 20$ $4 \times 5 = 20$
Lining up in pairs	12 people are lining up in 2s. $2 + 2 + 2 + 2 + 2 + 2 = 12$ $2 \times 6 = 12$

might model written calculations in naturally occurring situations. This emergent approach, however, will only be effective in a learning culture which fully embraces its philosophy and in an environment which promotes and supports risk taking, independence, enquiry and the desire of its learners to 'be mathematicians'. This approach can be facilitated by one's day-to-day practice and continuous provision, such as the playful contexts offered in role play, play trays and small world dramas (see Chapter 2).

Ways to promote this include:

- Ensuring that adults use the many opportunities that exist during the day, including interaction with independent activities, to model ways of recording mathematics and to include the use of formal symbols where appropriate and with explanation.

- Making available well-stocked collections of things with which to explore schematic play, such as baskets of shells, buttons, bricks and so on.

- Having a well-stocked graphics area with an abundance of attractive and varied mark-making resources (see Chapter 2).

- Providing clipboards and paper beside play trays and small world dramas to facilitate the spontaneous mark-making during or on reflection of play in these contexts.

- Displaying children's graphics and giving children ownership of presenting their own marks.

- Providing a range of opportunities for children to make mathematical graphics in both focused teaching sessions and in their independent play.

- Standing back and allowing children to explore their own marks, resisting the need to demand a 'right answer'.

- Avoiding telling the children what to do and building on a philosophy of sustained shared thinking.

- Being patient and promoting a positive, enquiring and mathematics-rich environment.

Introducing a time during the week in which to work with a small focused teaching group where children can 'have a go' at recording their own marks is an unthreatening way to begin. If the children have been accustomed to recording their mathematics in more formal ways, they might find the freedom of the empty whiteboard and the invitation to 'have a go' inhibiting at first. With gentle encouragement and by ensuring that the learning environment promotes a positive culture in which children feel they can take risks, many of them will begin to find the empty whiteboard liberating.

 Creative ideas for good practice

Context: small focused teaching group

Objective: multiplication as repeated addition

Resources: *Handa's Surprise* by Eileen Browne (see Resources); 4 play people; basket of 8 satsumas; whiteboards; pens; individual number lines

Begin with a very brief retelling of the story of Handa's arrival in the village with her basket of satsumas. Use the small world props to help create a visual image during the retelling. Explain that Handa is going to give each of the play people 2 satsumas, use the small world props to illustrate and ask the children to discuss what they notice. Then suggest: 'Handa would now like each person to have 3 satsumas. How can you calculate how many there will be? How could you work it out? If you want to use your whiteboard, what marks, drawings or symbols could you use? Talk to someone near you about how you might begin'. Give the children time to discuss their thoughts before they record. Remind them that any drawings should be 'maths drawings' to help their mathematical thought. Ask them to discuss what they have done and why. Use observations to help inform what, if any, are the misconceptions that need addressing and what are the next steps for each child.

What happens to the mathematical graphics?

In the early days of encouraging mathematical graphics, often more recording on paper is produced than necessary. Offering children whiteboards reduces the amount of paper used. Whiteboards are probably best used in focused teaching sessions where the practitioner can keep a close eye on what is being recorded, and if required can photocopy the marks produced before the board is cleaned. Providing whiteboards in role play and by play trays will certainly encourage children to mark-make but provides little opportunity for the marks to be kept as children joining the area will clean them ready for their own use. Mathematical graphics recorded on paper can be:

- displayed by the child on the children's own display board, thus giving them ownership of the process (see Chapter 2)

- shown by the child at review time (see Chapter 8), discussed and evaluated

- annotated and included in the child's learning journey, portfolio or maths folder

- kept in a class folder to illustrate to parents and others the work explored over a specific period.

Suggested further reading

Anning, A. and Ring, K. (2004) *Making Sense of Children's Drawings.* Maidenhead: OUP.

Atkinson, S. (ed.) (1992) *Mathematics with Reason.* London: Hodder & Stoughton.

Brizuela, B. (2004) *Mathematical Development in Young Children: Exploring Notations.* Colombia University: Teachers College Press.

Carruthers, E. and Worthington, M. (2006) *Children's Mathematics: Making Marks, Making Meaning,* 2nd edition. London: Sage Publications.

DCSF (2008) *Independent Review of Mathematics Teaching in Early Years Settings and Primary Schools.* London: DCSF.

DCSF (2008) *Mark Making Matters: Young Children Making Meaning in all areas of Learning and Development.* Nottingham: DCSF.

Gifford, S. (2005) *Teaching Mathematics 3–5: Developing Learning in the Foundation Stage.* Buckingham: OUP.

Hall, N. and Robinson, A. (2003) *Exploring Writing and Play in the Early Years,* 2nd edition. London: David Fulton Publishers.

See also, www.childrens-mathematics.net

Counting and using number

> **This chapter covers:**
> - the development of counting skills, and how this can be supported
> - the imaginative use of number lines and counting sticks
> - early mathematical operations
> - using money
> - examples of focused teaching activities and recorded work, along with examples of independent activities based on the theme of 'the farm'.

Counting

Learning to count proficiently involves the acquisition of skills through involvement in key experiences using the language of number and comparison (Montague-Smith, 2002). Children need to:

- learn number names in order

- count objects by touching them

- understand that the last number they say is the total number of objects in the group

- transfer these skills effectively from one context to the next

- move competently from counting concrete objects to counting abstractly.

It is crucial to provide a wide range of interesting objects, both like and unlike, for children to count and to ensure that there is a purpose for the activity, whether for the sheer joy of handling and observing tiny shells in a basket, or finding the number of play people that will fit into a vehicle made in the construction area. The practitioner must, therefore, plan carefully to ensure that the learning environment offers opportunities for counting in stimulating and meaningful ways (see Examples below).

Boxes and baskets, filled with interesting objects, can be displayed on table-tops to encourage children to observe, feel and count. The contents of these counting collections might include:

Photo 4.1   Harvesting these apples in a nearby orchard provides real opportunities for counting in 10s.

- acorns

- beads

- butter beans (that can become 'magic beans' by spray-painting them)

- buttons

- clothes pegs

- dog biscuits

- conkers

- glass pebbles/marbles

- leaves

- pasta shapes (again can be spray-painted)

- salt dough objects (theme-related)

- shells

- sunflower/pumpkin seeds.

This is most successful when these counting collections are changed frequently and are related to the current theme and interests of the youngsters. Children also need to explore the equivalence of number, and have opportunities to count in 2s, 5s, and 10s (see Examples below). Counting a large number of objects in 10s, for example, allows them to explore a 'big number', and also provides children with valuable experience in preparing for place value.

There is generally an over-emphasis on the cardinal nature of number in the early years (Haylock and Cockburn, 2003). When planning artefacts for counting boxes and baskets, it is also valuable to create opportunities for children to order numbers, examples being:

- matching the number of spots on a salt dough ladybird to the corresponding numeral on leaves numbered 0–10 placed alongside

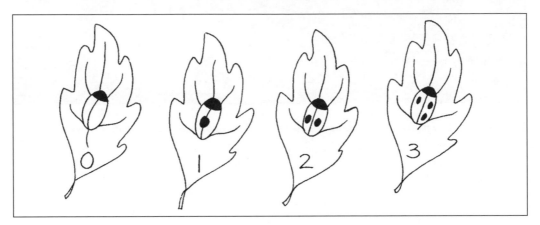

Figure 4.1   Matching number of spots to corresponding numeral

- placing the corresponding number of plastic flies on 'webs' (made of paper and string) numbered 0–10

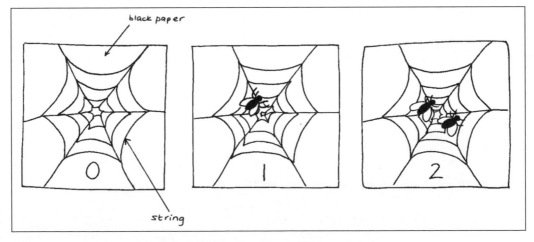

Figure 4.2   Matching number of spiders to corresponding numeral

- placing numbered model houses in numerical order.

Specific number apparatus such as Numicon® (see Resources), along with number lines and objects, allow children to explore the 'threeness of 3', for example.

Using number lines

Much is written about the value of young children's involvement with number lines in their mathematical development (Haylock and Cockburn, 2003; Pound, 1999; Worthington and Carruthers, 2003). Indeed, Haylock and Cockburn (2003: 26) suggest:

> '... young children should do as much of their number work moving up and down number lines, or similar manifestations of the ordinal aspect, as they do manipulating sets of counters and blocks'.

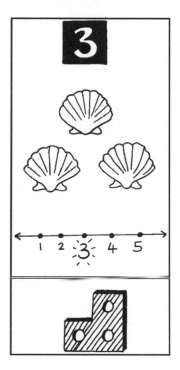

Figure 4.3   Number of interest

Young children should have access to number lines in all their forms. These include:

- number tracks

- number snakes (number tracks in the form of a snake often going up to numbers beyond 20)

- washing lines accompanied by baskets of numeral cards and pegs

- individual tracks and lines (for use with fingers or counters)

- big floor number lines and tracks (for jumping along)

- counting sticks.

Big floor number lines are particularly useful as they enable children to count the jumps they make forwards, or back along the number line, and help them experience the ordinal system in a very physical way. Some younger children find this easier than manipulating fingers or objects along smaller, individual number lines.

There are several ways of making number lines (Tucker, 2001b). These might include:

- numerals and line attached to a plastic carpet runner

- carpet tape stuck to indoor flooring to create a permanent number line

- number line sewn onto a long roll of hessian

- 'instant' number line using a roll of thick ribbon and numeral cards or tiles

- permanently marked number lines in the outside area.

They can be used imaginatively in practitioner-intensive sessions:

- featuring in maths stories as stepping stones to cross, for example

- as reference points to illustrate the connections between the ordinal and cardinal nature of number

- showing connections between the different structures of addition and subtraction (see below).

By ensuring that number lines are constantly available, both indoors and outdoors, and by allowing children time and space for their exploration, they are often incorporated into the children's own play. Such examples of their use might include:

- as numbered parking areas

- as house/shop numbers

- as rivers and stepping stones

- during children's own games with dice and other objects.

This allows children to make important connections between experience in their play and the understanding of the number system.

Counting sticks

In effect, the counting stick is a form of the blank number line. Demarcated with lines at regular intervals, it is the ideal resource for counting on, or back, from any given number, counting in given units and problem solving. Commonly used throughout the primary school, it can be put to good effect in the early years in conjunction with a small puppet in a story context (see Table 8.1). By ascribing the beginning of the stick with a number, the children can count on and back in given units. It offers excellent opportunities for the use of mathematical vocabulary and problem solving. Prompts might include:

Figure 4.4 Counting stick

- What number has the puppet landed on?

- How do you know?

- Can you show the same number of fingers?

- What number comes before/after?

- How many more jumps will the puppet need to get to the end?

- How many more jumps will the puppet need to go back to the beginning?

- If the puppet starts at 0, how many jumps of 2 will it need to get to 10?

As with number lines, the counting stick can be made available to children to incorporate in their own play. By providing finger puppets (frogs, caterpillars, etc.), children can retell stories from focused teaching sessions, and develop their own. Supplies of 'post-it' notes are also useful for children to write numerals on and label the counting stick as they wish.

 Creative ideas for good practice

In order to promote the use of mathematical vocabulary:

- model mathematics vocabulary during daily routines and in focused teaching
- allow children time and space to use mathematical vocabulary during focused teaching sessions and encourage them to practise using these 'new' words in their independent play
- encourage the use of the 'micro-chat', where children are encouraged to talk quietly to a partner about a specific mathematical problem. This engages every child in the activity and gives them all time to speak in sentences.

Mathematical operations

The most commonly used mathematical operations in the early years are summarized in Table 4.1, Examples of mathematical operations in playful contexts.

Important points to consider when teaching mathematical operations are:

- Avoid over-emphasis on particular mathematical structures, typically addition as the union of two sets and subtraction as take away. Frequently, over-emphasis on some structures, such as take away, occur to the exclusion of all others (Haylock and Cockburn, 2003).

- Use number lines to highlight connections between activities and mathematical structures, such as jumping back along a number line to exemplify reduction (see Activity 4.3: 'Eating aphids').

Table 4.1   Examples of mathematical operations in playful contexts

Mathematical operation	Structure	Example of practitioner's question in specific learning context
Addition	• Union of two sets • Counting on	• Role play: 'Claire has 2 post bags, 1 of which has 3 letters and the other 2 letters. How many letters does Claire have altogether?' • Play tray: 'How many scoops of corn did it take to fill the sack? Samira put in 4, then 3 more'.
Subtraction	• Taking away (partitioning) • Counting back (reduction) • Difference (comparison) • Inverse of addition (complementary addition)	• Washing line: 'There are 6 sacks on the washing line. Jayesh takes 3 down. How many are left?' • Number line (on a big leaf number line 0–10) 'The ladybird is on leaf number 8. It flies 4 leaves back. Where will it land?' • Block play: 'Tilly has made her ice-cream stall with 8 wooden blocks. Sam has made his with 6. How many more wooden blocks did Tilly use?' • Role play: 'The baker must have 12 cakes on the shelf. She has already made 4, so how many more does she need to make?'
Multiplication	• Repeated addition • Scaling	• Play tray: 'I can see 4 plant pots with 2 spiders in each one. How many spiders are there altogether?' • Block play (using same sized blocks): 'Joe's wall is 4 blocks long. Chloe wants to make a wall 2 times as long. How many blocks does she need?'
Division	• Repeated subtraction • Sharing • Grouping (inverse of multiplication)	• Role play (using a plate of 6 biscuits): 'How many times can we take 2 biscuits?' • Role play: 'We have 3 children and 9 items of washing to do. Can you share out the washing fairly?' • Malleable materials: 'How many bags of 2 bread buns do we need to make 10 bread buns?'

Using money

Some early years settings and schools have differing views about using real money for teaching and learning and it is up to individual settings to establish their own guidelines about this. Undoubtedly, there are benefits in allowing children to handle, and consequently familiarize themselves, with real coins, giving the activities in which they are involved authenticity. Possibilities for play involving money in specific areas in the learning environment might include:

- role play – using money in 'real-life' situations

- modelling and painting – printing with coins, coin rubbings, moulds in modelling dough

- play trays – sorting coins into a selection of unusual/attractive purses or bags

- construction/technology – making simple money boxes big enough for 10 coins

- table-top counting activities – counting pennies in a 'staircase'; counting pennies in groups of 10; laying coins in a pattern.

Such experiences provide opportunities to familiarize children with the shape, colour and size of each coin in contexts that promote the use of related vocabulary: coin, value, amount, worth more, worth less, greater than, too expensive, less expensive, cheaper than. Only when children are able to identify and name coins confidently are they ready to begin to make amounts. Exchange games are a useful precursor to this. The most successful of these are simply made by the practitioner or the children themselves and depict their current interests. With the use of dice, children can collect specified numbers of pennies which are then exchanged for a given coin, such as exchanging five pennies for a 5p coin.

Examples of activities

Activity 4.1   Bags of Biscuits

Learning objective:	Recognition of cardinal numbers.
Resources:	Numeral cards 0–10; salt dough biscuits; newsprint paper 'cones' (to act as simple bags); coloured pens; large floor number line.
How to begin:	Ask a group of children to help bag up 'butter biscuits' for the farm shop. The shop is going to sell them in bags of different quantities. Ask each child to take a numeral card and read out the numeral. This is the number of biscuits they will count out and put into their bag. Once the biscuits are bagged, the child draws a picture (array) of the number of biscuits within, or writes the corresponding numeral on a piece of paper and sticks this on to the bag. Allow the children to fill two or three bags.
Development:	Ask the children to swap bags to check that the biscuits have been counted accurately by taking their bag to the corresponding numeral on a large floor number line. Encourage the children to take out the biscuits and lay them in a column above the numeral to count and check. Doing this for all the numerals along the number line helps to reinforce the connection between cardinal and ordinal numbers, and provides a clear visual image of the growing nature of numbers 0–10.
Key vocabulary:	Number names 0–10; enough; not enough; too many; too few; more than; greater than; less than; fewer than; in a line; order; group; set.
Simplification:	Use number cards, or tiles, 0–5.
Extension:	Children are told that the biscuits are to be bagged in 10s. Using random numeral cards 10–30, children work in pairs to collect a numeral card, identify the numeral upon it and count out the number in groups of 10. Each group of 10 is bagged with the numeral written upon it. Encourage the children to say how many groups of 10 and how many left over their numeral has. The bags of 10, and few remaining unbagged biscuits, provide a clear visual image of 10s and 1s.

Activity 4.2   Ladybird Friends

Learning objective:	Addition of two groups.
Resources:	Green paper leaves; sets of paper ladybirds with spots 0–10 (one set per child); large floor number line 0–10; writing materials.
How to begin:	Tell the children a story about ladybirds helping the farmers by eating the aphids on the crops. The ladybirds have always been happy to hunt for aphids on their own, but today they want to go with a friend. The friend they will go with is the ladybird with spots that gives them 10 spots in all. Children arrange pairs of ladybirds on each leaf, ensuring that their spots add up to 10.
Development:	Ask the children to discuss which mathematical graphics they could use to represent each pairing, and then to record their thoughts. Each child will have a ladybird remaining with five spots. Ask what they might do to help this one. Encourage the children to see the connection between the counting on and union of two sets by 'jumping' their mark-making or algorithm along the number line. Discuss their mathematical graphics and any misconceptions they might have.
Key vocabulary:	Number names 0–10; how many more; add; makes; equals; is the same as.
Simplification:	Use sets of ladybirds 0–5. Ask the children to select their own criteria for finding a friend in order to begin relating addition to combining two groups of spots.
Extension:	Use ladybirds with spots 0–20 and ask the children to combine spots to add up to 20.

Activity 4.3   Eating Aphids

Learning objective:	Understanding of the operation of subtraction and the related vocabulary.
Resources:	'Aphids' (plastic flies or laminated paper drawings); plastic or paper ladybird; large floor number line 0–10; individual number lines 0–10; writing materials.
How to begin:	Tell the children a variety of subtraction stories, giving them the opportunity to manipulate the resources with the storytelling. Stories might include: The ladybird eats 4 aphids. How many are left?' The ladybird ate 3 aphids yesterday and 7 aphids this morning. What is the number difference between the 2 amounts?' The ladybird wants to eat 10 aphids by the end of the day. It has eaten 3 already. How many more does it need to eat to make 10?'
Development:	Offer the children opportunities to discuss and record mathematical graphics to illustrate each subtraction story. Ask the children to use the number line to make connections between taking away examples and the reduction structure of subtraction.

Key vocabulary:	Subtraction; take away; less than; how many are left?; count back; equals; is the same as; difference; how many more to make.
Simplification:	Use five aphids and reinforce by encouraging children to use materials, fingers and number lines with each example and alongside associated vocabulary.
Extension:	Ask children to record the corresponding algorithm as both addition and subtraction.

Activity 4.4   Frog And Lily Pads

Learning objective:	Repeated addition.
Resources:	Number tiles 2, 3, 4, 6; big floor number line 0–12; individual number lines 0–12; big plastic frog; 13 paper lily pads; small plastic frogs (1 per child); writing materials.
How to begin:	Tell a story about a frog who likes to jump across the pond to the farm in different ways – in jumps of 2s, 3s, 4s or 6s. Ask a child to place a lily pad beside each numeral on the big number line. This will be the way across the pond. In turn, each child is the frog. Holding the big frog, the child picks up a number tile, identifies the numeral on it and says how he or she will be jumping across the pond today. The child jumps along the number line, 'resting' on each multiple of the chosen number to highlight the pattern that emerges. Meanwhile, the other members of the group are involved by jumping their small frog in the same way along their individual number lines.
Development:	Children discuss and record mathematical graphics in a simple 'diary' showing how the frog jumps each day:

Tom has drawn the pond with 'number line' lilypads going across He has marked the numerals 0, 2, 4, 6, 8, 10, 12 and talked about the frog missing a number out each time

Figure 4.5   Tom (R) can count in twos

(Continued)

(Continued)

Figure 4.6   Nita (Y1) recognizes that more than two numbers can be added together

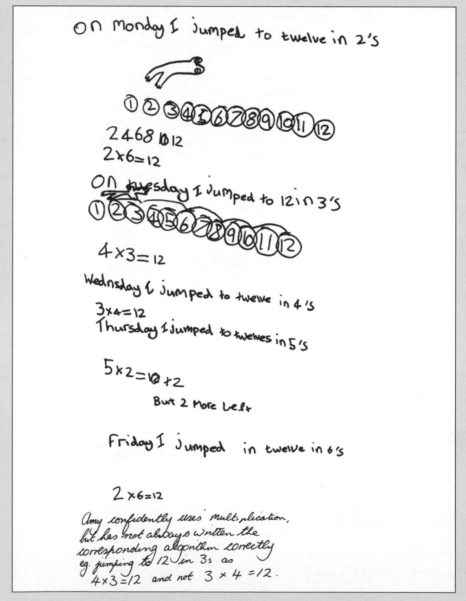

Figure 4.7   Amy (Y2) can represent multiplication as repeated addition

	'On Monday the frog jumps across the pond like this ...'; 'On Tuesday ...'
Key vocabulary:	Jumps of; the same; equal numbers; adding; the same again; repeated; how many jumps altogether?; makes; equals; is the same as.
Simplification:	Use big number line 0–10 and explore jumping in 2s. Use individual number tracks rather than number lines.
Extension:	Children record algorithms as multiplication.

 Principles into practice

- Provide interesting and varied objects for children to count in meaningful situations.
- Encourage children to make links between the cardinal and ordinal nature of number.
- Use number lines frequently and make them available for children to use for reference, and to incorporate into their own play.
- Ensure children have opportunities to see and discuss the different structures of mathematical operations, avoiding over-emphasis on one.
- Model mathematical vocabulary and recording, using standard notation where appropriate.

Suggested further reading

Anghileri, J. (2000) *Teaching Number Sense*. London: Continuum.

Cockburn, A.D. (2008) *Mathematics Misconceptions*. London: Sage Publications.

Cooke, H. (2007) Mathematics for Primary and Early Years, 2nd edition. London: Sage Publications.

Haylock, D. and Cockburn, A. (2008) *Understanding Mathematics for Young Children*, 3rd edition. London: Sage Publications.

Montague-Smith, A. (2002) *Mathematics in Nursery Education*, 2nd edition. London: David Fulton Publishers.

Mosley, F. (2001) *Using Number Lines*. London: Beam Education.

Pepperell, S., Hopkins, C., Gifford, S. and Tallent, T. (2009) *Mathematics in the Primary School: A Sense of Progression*. London: Routledge.

Thompson, I. (ed.) (2008) *Teaching and Learning Early Number*, 2nd edition. Berkshire: Open University Press.

Examples of independent activities: The farm

Example 4.1   Animal homes

Learning context: small world drama
Learning objectives:

- In practical activities and discussion, begin to use the vocabulary involved in adding (ELG)
- Recall doubles of all numbers to at least 10 (PNS YI)
- Understand that halving is the inverse of doubling (PNS Y2)

	FS	Y1	Y2
Activity	Children count the animals already set up in a row in a field. Reproduce a second row of animals in the field and check the total by counting on. Develop small world role play.	Children take a 'market ticket'. They double the number shown and count out this number of animals into the field. Record the number taken and its double. Develop small world role play.	Children take a 'farm ticket' and halve the number shown. They count out this number of animals and put them in a field. Record the operation using appropriate symbols. Develop small world role play.
Resources	Green cloth; sticks; pebbles; bark (for enclosure making); play people; selection of plastic farm animals; farm buildings; river (blue fabric).	In addition to FS: pack of 'market tickets' (numeral cards 1–5); clipboard and writing materials.	In addition to FS: pack of 'market tickets' (numeral cards 2–20); clipboard and writing materials.
Prompt and key questions	The farmer has not got enough animals to take to market. Count the number of animals in a row and make another row exactly the same. How many animals are there altogether? Is the number greater or smaller now you have added more?	The farmer is getting some animals ready to take to market, but the market tickets are wrong. The farmer needs to double the number of animals on each ticket. Can you work out the double of each number and put the correct number of animals in each field? Can you record this for the farmer's records?	The farmer is getting some animals ready for market, but the market tickets are wrong. The farmer needs to halve the number on the ticket. Can you work out the half of each number and put the correct number of animals in each field? Can you find ways to record this for the farmer?
Key vocabulary	• counting on • more than • altogether	• more than • double • half • addition	• half • double • less than • division
Opportunities for assessment	• can count out specified number accurately • uses vocabulary of counting • uses counting on to check total	• understands the concept of 'double' • can calculate double by manipulating objects/ quick mental recall uses + and = signs accurately to record response	• shows understanding of halving • can calculate half by manipulating objects/ quick mental recall uses ÷ sign accurately to record response

Example 4.2   Building tractor sheds

Learning context: construction area
Learning objectives:

- Count reliably up to 10 everyday objects (ELG)
- Estimate a number that can be checked by counting (PNS YI)
- Estimate a number of objects (PNS Y2)

	FS	Y1	Y2
Activity	Children estimate how many large wooden blocks it will take to house a ride-on/toy tractor. Construct shed, test with tractor, then count blocks. Record estimate and actual number in chosen method. Develop related role play.	Children estimate how many wooden bricks/Duplo® it will take to build a tractor shed for a toy tractor. Record estimate. Construct shed, test with tractor and count number of bricks used. Record number used. Develop related role play.	As Y1, but using Lego®.
Resources	Large wooden blocks; ride-on/large toy tractor; writing materials.	Small wooden bricks/Duplo®; small toy tractor; clipboard and writing materials.	Lego®; small toy tractor; clipboard and writing materials.
Prompt and key questions	Can you help the farmer build a shed for the tractor? How many wooden blocks do you think you will need? How many did you use? Was your guess right? Which number was the biggest: your guess or the number you used? Was the number you guessed and the number you used the same?	Can you help the farmer build a shed for the tractor? Can you estimate how many wooden bricks/pieces of Duplo® you will need? Can you record your estimate and the actual number of bricks used? Which is greatest, or do your recordings show equal numbers?	Can you help the farmer build a shed for the tractor? Estimate and record how many pieces of Lego® you will need. Which is greatest: your estimate or the actual number of bricks used, or are they equal numbers? What is the difference between your estimate and the actual number of bricks?
Key vocabulary	• guess (estimate) • vocabulary of number • more than/greater than • less than/smaller than • the same	• estimate • accurate • more than/less than • equal numbers	• estimate • actual • accurate • equal numbers
Opportunities for assessment	• uses vocabulary of number • can make a sensible guess (estimate) • shows an understanding of more than/less than • can recognize when two numbers are equal	• makes a sensible estimate • can count objects accurately • can recognize when two numbers are equal	• makes a sensible estimate • can talk about difference

Example 4.3   Egg boxes

Learning context: malleable materials
Learning objectives:

- Use developing mathematical ideas and methods to solve practical problems (ELG)
- Understand subtraction as 'take away' and find a 'difference' by 'counting up' (PNS YI)
- Understand that subtraction is the reverse of addition and vice versa (PNS Y2)

	FS	Y1	Y2
Activity	Children count modelling dough eggs already placed in an egg box. Children calculate by counting how many more are needed to make 6. Use modelling dough to make required number of eggs and place in egg box to fill. Explore dough with fingers and tools.	As FS, but children record results.	As Y1, but record results as subtraction.
Resources	Egg boxes (already containing a given number of made eggs); modelling dough.	In addition to FS: clipboard and writing materials.	As Y1.
Prompt and key questions	Some of the eggs have been broken. Can you work out how many more eggs you need to fill the box? How many eggs have you made? How many eggs are there altogether now?	Some of the eggs have been broken. Can you work out how many more eggs you need to fill the box and make a record for the egg packers of what you have done?	As Y1, and also can you record what you have done for the egg packers as an addition and subtraction statement?
Key vocabulary	• how many more to make? • altogether • add • count on	• how many more to make? • difference	• how many more to make? • addition • subtraction • difference
Opportunities for assessment	• uses vocabulary of number • can count on from a given number • can calculate how many more are needed	• can calculate how many more are needed • can record response using – and = symbols	• understands relationship between addition and subtraction • can record response using – and = symbols

Example 4.4   The farm shop

Learning context: role play
Learning objectives:

- Sort objects, making choices and justifying decisions (PNS FS)
- Solve problems involving money, for example to 'pay' and 'give change' (PNS Y1)
- Solve problems involving addition in contexts of pounds and pence (PNS Y2)

	FS	Y1	Y2
Activity	Children sort coins into shop till. Develop role play.	Children select and buy goods up to the value of 20p, giving change where necessary. Develop role play.	Children calculate 'takings' in the till and enter the sum in the 'accounts book' using £.p notation.
Resources	Shop till; coins 1p to £2; cheque book; credit card; priced goods up to 20p, telephone; calendar; 'order book'; writing materials; purses; bags; paper bags; bucket balance; dressing-up clothes.	As FS.	In addition to FS: 'accounts book'.
Prompt and key questions	The till needs preparing for the day. Can you sort the coins into the till? Which coins do you have the most/fewest of?	After a visit to the farm, you can buy a treat up to the value of 20p. What coins will you use to make the value of your purchase? Do you need any change? How much change will you need? How did you calculate that?	When the shop closes, we need to calculate the day's takings. Can you record this in the accounts book using £.p notation? How much was taken? How did you record that?
Key vocabulary	• value names of coins • value • amount	• value names of coins • value • amount • purchase • more expensive • cheaper than • change	• total amount • sum of • pounds and pence
Opportunities for assessment	• can sort for like coins • uses vocabulary of money • uses vocabulary of counting	• recognizes and names all coins to at least 20p • can make values to 20p • can calculate change from 20p	• calculates total amount accurately • correctly uses £.p notation

Example 4.5   Hay bale sheds

Learning context: small world drama
Learning objectives:

- Begin to relate addition to combing two groups of objects (ELG)
- Derive and recall all pairs of numbers with a total of 10 (PNS YI)
- Derive and recall all addition facts for each number to at least 10 and all pairs with totals of 20 (PNS Y2)

	FS	Y1	Y2
Activity	Children use materials to construct 2 enclosures. Place 5 bales in the 2 enclosures. Draw representation for farmer's records. Develop small world play.	Children use materials to construct 2 enclosures and find as many ways as they can of storing 10 bales between them. Record their findings. Develop small world play.	As for Y1, but using 20 'hay bales'.
Resources	Selection of plastic farm animals; toy tractors; twigs; pebbles; bark; etc. (for enclosure making); play people; 5 'hay bales' (small cubes of sponge); clipboard and writing materials.	As FS, but using 10 'hay bales'.	As FS, but using 20 'hay bales'.
Prompt and key questions	The farmer needs to store some hay bales in 2 sheds. Can you build 2 sheds and find how the 5 bales could be stored? Are there always 5 bales altogether? How many different ways can you find? Can you find a way of making a record for the farmer showing the ways you have found?	The farmer needs to store 10 hay bales in 2 sheds. Can you build 2 sheds and find, and record, as many ways as you can of storing the bales? Are all the ways you have found different? How many ways did you find? What do you notice about your records?	The farmer needs to store 20 hay bales in 2 sheds. Can you find, and record, all the ways the bales can be stored? How many different ways are there? What do you notice about your results?
Key vocabulary	• vocabulary of number • add • more than/greater than • altogether	• addition • more than/greater than • pairs of numbers	• more than/greater than • addition facts
Opportunities for assessment	• uses vocabulary of number • can count total number of objects • can record pictorially/ uses + and = symbols	• can calculate by manipulating objects/quick recall of known number facts • can record using + and = symbols accurately	• can calculate by manipulating objects/ quick recall of known number facts • can record using + and = symbols accurately

Example 4.6   Pricing for the farm shop

Learning context: graphics area
Learning objectives:

- Reognize numerals 1 to 9 (ELG)
- Solve problems involving money (PNS YI)
- Sovle problems involving subtraction in contexts of pounds and pence (PNS Y2)

	FS	Y1	Y2
Activity	Children select materials and use simple tools to make price tags for goods in the farm shop. Explore tools and mark-making.	Children design and make a poster advertising goods in the farm shop. Using a given 'price list', children transfer prices onto their poster in order of value.	Children design and make a poster advertising reduced goods. Using a given 'price list', they subtract 50p from each price, showing the new price on the poster.
Resources	Card; paper; scissors; hole punch; pieces of string/ribbon; coloured pens and pencils.	Coloured paper; coloured pens and pencils; 'price list' (apple pie 90p, ice-cream tub 70p, jam 80p, biscuits 45p, fudge 50p ...).	Coloured paper; coloured pens and pencils; 'price list' (flower pots £1.70, bread baskets £2, butter biscuits £1, honey £1.90 ...).
Prompt and key questions	Can you make some price tags for things in the farm shop? Which goods are the labels for and how much are they? Which is the most/least expensive?	We need some posters advertising goods to put in the farm shop. Can you design and make a poster listing the things on the price list in order of value? Which is the most/least expensive? What is the difference in price between the most and least expensive item?	We need some posters advertising reduced goods in the farm shop. All the goods on the price list are reduced by 50p. Can you design and make a poster showing how much the goods have been reduced by, along with their new price? What did you do to calculate the new price? Which is the most/least expensive? What is the difference in price between the most and least expensive item?
Key vocabulary	• price • amount • value • most expensive • least expensive	• most expensive • least expensive • value • amount • difference in price	• most expensive • least expensive • difference in price • reduced
Opportunities for assessment	• uses vocabulary of money • can read price tags made • can identify greatest/least value shown on tags	• reads amounts on 'price list' • orders amounts accurately	• can explain method used to calculate new price • accurately uses £.p notation

Example 4.7   Sheep for shearing

Learning context: washing line
Learning objectives:

- Say and use number names in order in familiar contexts (ELG)
- Use knowledge of place value to position numbers 0–20 on a number track and number line (PNS Y1)
- Order two-digit numbers and position them on a number line (PNS Y2)

	FS	Y1	Y2
Activity	Children peg 11 card sheep, each marked with a numeral 0–10, along a washing line. Develop related narrative/ small world play.	Children peg 20 card sheep marked with a numeral 0–20 along a washing line. Develop related narrative/small world play.	Children peg 20 card sheep marked with random numbers 0–100 along a washing line.
Resources	Laminated card sheep each marked with a coloured numeral 0–10; clothes pegs; washing line; simple picture of a barn (to peg at the end of the ordered sheep); basket of small world farm toys.	As FS, but with 21 card sheep marked with numerals 0–20.	As FS, but with 20 card sheep marked with random numerals between 0 and 100.
Prompt and key questions	The farmer needs to take the sheep in order to the barn for shearing. Can you peg the sheep in order along the washing line? Which number is first/last? Which sheep comes in between 5 and 7? etc.	The farmer needs to take the sheep in order to the barn for shearing. Can you peg the sheep in numerical order? Which number is first/last? Which sheep comes in between 15 and 17? etc.	The farmer has missed out some of the sheep for shearing. Can you peg the missing sheep in numerical order along the washing line? Which sheep has the greatest/smallest number?
Key vocabulary	• number names • order • more than/greater than • smaller than/less than • in between	• numerical order • more than/greater than • less than/smaller than • in between	• numerical order • more than/greater than • less than/smaller than • in between
Opportunities for assessment	• recognizes and names numerals 0–10 • uses vocabulary of number • uses vocabulary of more than/less than • orders numerals 0–10 accurately	• recognizes and names numerals 0–20 • orders numerals 0–20 accurately • identifies numbers in between two given numbers	• recognizes and names given numerals 0–100 • displays understanding of place value

Example 4.8   The pond

Learning context: play tray
Learning objectives:

- Count reliably up to 10 everyday objects (ELG) and count in 2s (PNS FS)
- Count reliably at least 20 objects, recognizing that when rearranged the number of objects stays the same (PNS Y1)
- Count up to 100 objects by grouping them and counting in 10s (PNS Y2)

	FS	Y1	Y2
Activity	Children count out 2 frogs and place on each lily pad. Count total number of frogs in 2s. Develop small world play.	Children use net to pond dip. Count number of creatures caught with each dip and record on a clipboard. Develop small world play.	Children count flies in groups of 10. Count in 10s to find total number of flies altogether. Record findings on a clipboard.
Resources	Green 'pond' water (green food colouring); 10 plastic frogs; 5 'lily pads' (green fabric); plastic pond creatures (newts, water snails, tadpoles); 'frog spawn' (circular pieces of bubble wrap); pieces of wood/bark; pebbles.	In addition to FS: small fishing net; clipboard and writing materials.	In addition to FS: 100 plastic flies.
Prompt and key questions	The frogs like to sit in pairs. Can you put 2 frogs on each lily pad? How many frogs are there altogether?	Use the net to go pond dipping. Can you count how many creatures you catch with each dip, and record your results? Which dip had the greatest/fewest catch?	The frogs like to eat flies in groups of 10. Can you count out the flies in groups of 10? How many flies will the frogs eat altogether? How can you record this?
Key vocabulary	• vocabulary of number • count on • more than/greater than • pair	• vocabulary of number • more than/greater than • greatest/smallest	• tens • multiples
Opportunities for assessment	• counts out 2 accurately • uses vocabulary of numbers • successfully counts in 2s	• counts objects accurately • can record numerals • can order numbers recorded	• accurately groups in 10s • can count to 100 in 10s • can record pictorially/ as repeated addition/ as multiplication

5

Pattern

This chapter covers:

- pattern as a precursor to algebra
- understanding pattern
- patterns in the environment
- examples of focused teaching activities and recorded work, along with independent activities based on the theme of 'clothes'.

Pattern has often been under-represented in the early years mathematics curriculum and has not enjoyed the high profile that counting and using number have (Pound, 1999). Sadly, all too often, young children's experience of 'pattern work' consists of activities with pegs, beads and colouring in. Pattern, of course, exists way beyond the peg board and bead tray, and in its various forms can be seen, experienced and heard throughout daily life. In mathematics, pattern is concerned with the relationships between shapes and numbers and it is because of this that pattern is the precursor to algebra. Consequently, it is a fundamental aspect of early years mathematics. It is because of these relationships and connections that it can never be taught successfully as a 'stand-alone' unit of work. To do so would be to deprive young children of opportunities to make their own discoveries about pattern and to make meaningful connections between pattern and their everyday experiences.

Understanding pattern

Pattern is the arrangement of shapes, numbers and actions that follow given criteria. We can:

- see pattern (in shapes or numbers)

- hear pattern (in repeated sequences of music)

- feel pattern (clapping a pattern, or rhythm, or moving in a repeated sequence).

In order to be aware of and excited by pattern, young children should have the opportunity to discover, explore and create patterns in a variety of ways. Central to developing an understanding about pattern is children's ability to identify, sort for and discuss similarities and differences. They will also need to understand about order and have at their disposal language such as: first, next, after, before, in between, last. It is helpful to encourage children to clap a pattern that they have observed. For example, an ABAB pattern can be clapped, 'hands, knees, hands, knees' or an ABBA pattern, 'hands, knees, knees, hands'. This is beneficial in that it helps the children 'feel' the pattern, enabling them to understand how the similarities and differences they observe in one situation can be transferred to another. Indeed, Haylock and Cockburn (2003) suggest that when we consider number patterns what we are in fact doing is making a connection between the relationship between the numbers and a visual image. This is clearly seen when exploring odd and even numbers while counting out objects:

- When pairing the objects, the odd numbers are 'without a partner', while the even numbers all 'have a partner'.

- Numicon® plates representing an odd number have a piece 'sticking up', while the even number plates have a 'flat top'.

 Creative ideas for good practice

As part of a theme where children are folding clothes and blankets, or using tablecloths in their activities, unfold a square tablecloth or sheet to reveal the square, oblong, square, oblong shapes that emerge in a pattern with each unfolding. Encourage talk about the pattern. By clapping the hands, knees, hands, knees and saying the pattern 'square, oblong, square, oblong …', the children can make meaningful connections between the seeing, doing and saying of their pattern observation.

Patterns appear in different forms and can be grouped together as follows:

- **Repeated patterns**

  Children copy and create sequences, such as:

  – laying a toy ladybird, bee and spider in a line travelling into a plant pot in a small world drama, giving opportunities to talk about which minibeast is first, which is next and which is last, along with first, second and third. This sequence can then be repeated, and it is this understanding of making the sequence again and again and again that informs the child's understanding of pattern going on and on.

  – clapping a sequence of sounds, such as slow, quick, quick, and repeating this over again.

- **Increasing patterns**

  – Constructing number 'staircases', by placing the number of objects in a column above the corresponding numeral on a number line, illustrates the

Photo 5.1   These children are exploring the relationship between the cardinal and ordinal nature of number by making a shell 'staircase' along a hessian number line.

connection between the ordinal and cardinal aspects of number, and therefore the pattern in the number system itself.

- Using objects in conjunction with a number line in this way allows children to see clear images, for example of odd or even numbers where alternate columns of objects increase by two each time, and for doubles along a number line beyond 10.
- Allowing young children time and space to explore a large hundred square, either presented on a board they can handle, or on the floor, provides fantastic opportunities for them to spot patterns of numbers in columns, rows and diagonally. As with number lines, hundred squares made available in the graphics area and presented on large boards in the inside and outside environments encourage children to incorporate them into their own play.
- Increasing patterns can also be explored by constructing walls, stairs and platforms with construction kits, and columns of blocks, or pictograms in data-handling work.

- **Line patterns**

  - Objects from the natural world such as leaves and shells.
  - Fabric designs.
  - Works of art (see below).

Children can be encouraged to observe these and reproduce them using a variety of media: paint, clay, modelling dough or fabric and thread. Working with line patterns provides excellent opportunities to explore vocabulary such as: wavy, curved, zigzag, straight, bendy, arched, spiky, thick and thin, among others. This vocabulary can then act as 'movement' vocabulary, providing a basis for work in dance where the children use the words to stimulate a series of moves which are then repeated to create a sequence of movement. Percussion instruments can be used to accompany this, thus bringing together seeing pattern, moving pattern and hearing pattern.

Identifying pattern in the world around us

Pattern in art

Works of art are a fantastic stimulus for the exploration of pattern (see Resources). They provide a visual stimulus for children to copy or to inspire their own pattern making using a variety of media. Particularly useful works include:

- **Andy Goldsworthy**
  Photographs of his sculptures using natural materials act as great inspiration for children to construct their own sculptures in repeating patterns. They can be done on a large scale during a visit to the beach using shells, driftwood, seaweed and other natural materials, or in a large, flat play tray in the outside play area.

Photo 5.2 Stimulated by the sculptures of Andy Goldsworthy, this child is constructing repeating patterns using natural materials and glass beads.

They can also be achieved on a small scale using natural materials on pieces of black card.

- **Paul Klee**
  Much of Klee's work consists of pictures made with blocks of colour. This can inspire pictures made of colour patterns in paint, or applique work with fabric and thread.

- **William Morris**
  The repeating patterns featured in Morris' fabric and tiles provide ideas for young children and illustrate well how repeating patterns can work together to create a large piece of fabric, or cover a wall in tiles.

- **Bridget Riley**
  Her easily accessible paintings depict clear blocks of colour, often in repeating patterns.

- **Traditional African, Indian and Islamic art**
  These works of art often depict clear repeating patterns and line patterns. Indian pieces particularly often have clear repeating patterns around their borders.

Pattern in the learning environment

Practitioners can organize their learning environments to raise the profile of pattern through their displays, organization of resources and daily activities. By modelling pattern making, in the way resources are presented for example, practitioners can heighten the awareness of young children to pattern. Youngsters very soon realize that pattern is all around them and woven into their daily lives. By planning for and modelling pattern, practitioners are more likely to encourage children to become engaged in 'pattern spotting' and to be excited by it.

 Creative ideas for good practice

- Set out equipment, such as vehicles in the outside play area, in a repeated pattern such as lorry, bike, lorry, bike ...
- Provide interactive displays that can be changed regularly, such as:

  - big/small paper flowers
  - painted bees/butterflies
  - wide/narrow paper leaves
  - paper leaf/flower.

  All of these can be presented along a paper 'vine' which extends around the classroom. Other interactive displays might include:

  - a washing line on which to hang 'washing' in a different repeated pattern each day
  - flags (bunting) displayed in a colour or shape pattern.

- Introduce pattern into daily routines, such as giving things out in a pattern, asking children to line up in a pattern, looking for patterns in lunch or snack preferences.

Pattern in the natural world

The natural world also provides a rich source of pattern. Encouraging children to collect, observe and, where appropriate, print with a selection of leaves, shells and stones enables them to see that pattern is not always manufactured. It is also important to draw children's attention to the natural patterns of day and night and the cyclical pattern of the seasons. Animal life cycles are also important to consider.

Pattern in music and songs

Listening to music and music making provide many opportunities to identify and copy patterns. Children can:

- respond in movement to repeated rhythms they hear, and in a variety of media

- clap the rhythm of their name as they repeat their name over and over again and clap the syllables they hear

- use percussion instruments to create short, repeated rhythms and develop their own notation to record the quality of the patterns created.

There is a wealth of well-known and traditional songs which involve pattern, such as counting on and back in 2s or 1s ('Five currant buns') and increasing patterns ('One man went to mow'). There are many good mathematical song books available which include notes about the areas of mathematics they represent (see Resources). By making reference to a large number line during singing number songs, the practitioner can highlight the significance of pattern in each song, and help the children make valuable connections between the meaningful images the songs create for them, and patterns in the number system.

Examples of activities

Activity 5.1   Hanging out Clothes

Learning objective:	Identifying the pattern of counting in 2s and odd and even numbers.
Resources:	Washing line; clothes pegs; five small items of clothing (shorts, socks, hankies, etc.); large floor number line 0–10.
How to begin:	Tell the children that Mrs Mopple likes to hang out her washing using two pegs for each piece. She wants to find out how many pegs she will need to hang out her basketful of washing. Invite each child to hang out a piece of washing using two pegs. Ask the children how many pegs are used in all, encouraging them to count in 2s.
Development:	Ask each child to stand beside a different even numeral on the number line as they count 0, 2, 4, 6 and so on. Encourage them to discuss what they notice about their position on the number line. Highlight that they are standing on even numbers and ask them to clap the odd, even, odd, even pattern that emerges.
Key vocabulary:	Number names; how many?; odd; even; pairs; before; after; next.
Simplification:	Use numbers to 6.
Extension:	Ask the children to continue the pattern beyond 10 and to predict what would emerge.

Activity 5.2   Making Wrapping Paper

Learning objective: Making and describing patterns.

Resources: A selection of fabric from a variety of cultures depicting line and repeating patterns; squares of press print (or polystyrene); printing rollers; paper; paint; pencils.

How to begin: Ask the children to look at the fabric and to describe the shapes, colours and patterns they see. Ask them to identify and describe these repeating patterns and talk about their preferences with a friend. Invite them to design and make a printing block that can be used to make wrapping paper showing repeating patterns for the clothes shop.

Development: Ask the children to score a design on their press print using ideas from the fabric they have seen. Using paint, the children fill their paper with repeating patterns and describe their work, commenting on the shapes, colours and repeats they have used.

Key vocabulary: Swirl; curved; wavy, straight; zigzag; before; next; repeated.

Simplification: Use simple tools to print with, such as shells, corks, pine cones, string, etc.

Extension: Make two printing blocks and, using different colours, make different patterns on each row, describing the type of pattern they are, such as AABB, ABAB, ABBABB, etc.

Activity 5.3   Buying Clothes at the Clothes Shop

Learning objective: Seeing patterns in number calculations.

Resources: 10 sets of 10 items of clothing (either real or paper silhouettes); whiteboards and pens (1 per child); big floor number line 0–10; individual number lines 0–10.

How to begin: Ask the children to keep a record for the shop keeper of all the clothes sold. There are 10 items of clothing for sale on each 'shelf'. Ask a child to come and 'buy' 1 item of clothing from one of the piles and tell the group how many items are left in that pile. Ask the children to record the corresponding algorithm, or graphics, on their whiteboard. Invite a child to represent the algorithm $10 - 1 = 9$ on the big floor number line by starting at 10 and jumping

(Continued)

(Continued)

back 1. Other children can be involved by using their fingers to jump back on their individual number lines. This helps to make the connection between the take away and reduction structures of subtraction.

Development: Ask another child to 'buy' two items from the next pile, three items from the next and so on, asking the children to record the corresponding algorithm for each purchase. Encourage the children to discuss any patterns they notice (10 − 1 = 9, 10 − 2 = 8, 10 − 3 = 7, 10 − 4 = 6, etc.) and ask them if they can continue the patterns in their recording until all the clothes are 'sold'.

Key vocabulary.   Less than; more than; increase; decrease; subtract; equals; is the same as.

Extension: Ask the children to predict and record the pattern of sales that would emerge if two items of clothing were bought each time.

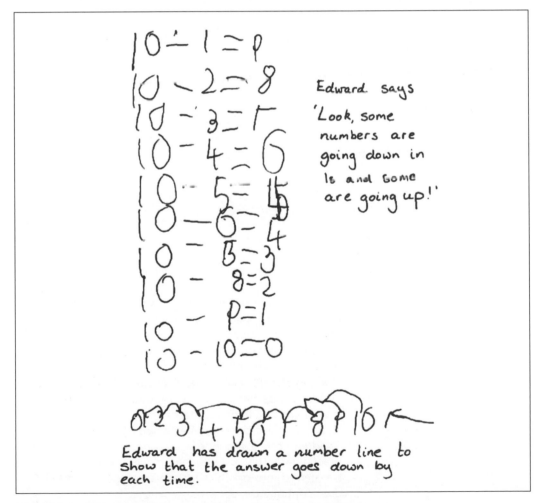

Figure 5.1   Edward (Y1) can use patterns of similar calculations

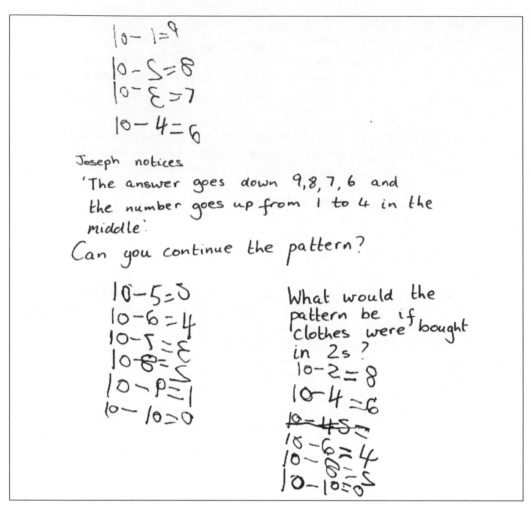

Figure 5.2   Joseph (Y2) uses patterns of similar calculations

Activity 5.4   Designing Clothes

Learning objective:	Making and describing patterns and pictures.
Resources:	A selection of percussion instruments; large paper cut-outs of items of clothing; drawing materials.
How to begin:	Encourage the children to explore the instruments and make simple repeated rhythms.
Development:	Ask the children to represent this sound pattern by drawing, using this pattern to decorate the cut-out clothing shapes. Encourage them to talk to a partner about their patterns and how they can change them to make rows of differing patterns.
Key vocabulary:	Curvy; straight; zigzag; swirly; sharp; thick; thin.
Simplification:	Children copy a simple repeated rhythm made by the practitioner. The practitioner models how this can be transferred into graphics on a paper cut-out, and children continue the pattern.

Examples of independent activities: Clothes

Example 5.1   Clothes shop

Learning context: construction area
Learning objectives:

- Talk about, recognize and recreate patterns (ELG)
- Describe simple patterns and relationships involving numbers or shapes (PNS YI)
- Describe patterns and relationships involving numbers or shapes, make predictions and test these with examples (PNS Y2)

	FS	Y1	Y2
Activity	Children use construction materials to build a 'clothes shop', laying construction materials in a pattern as they do so. Develop builders' role play.	As FS, but children also record a 'plan' of the building they construct.	As FS, but children begin by drawing a design of the building and pattern they are going to construct.
Resources	Large wooden blocks of varying sizes; plastic crates; clipboards; writing materials; builders' role-play resources.	A wide selection of small 3D solid shapes; clipboards and writing materials.	As Y1.
Prompt and key questions	Can you use the blocks to build a clothes shop? The owner wants the design of the shop front to show a pattern. How can you arrange the different blocks to show a pattern? What comes next/before/in between? Can you describe the pattern you have made? Can you draw your building?	Can you use the wooden blocks to build a clothes shop? The owner wants the design of the shop front to show a pattern. How can you construct your building? What shapes have you used? What sort of pattern is it? Can you draw your building and describe the pattern you have made for the owner?	The owner of a clothes shop wants you to draw a design for a new building using bricks in a pattern. Can you draw a design, then build the clothes shop? What bricks have you used? What sort of pattern is it? Why did you choose this pattern? Are there enough bricks to continue the pattern if you built another shop?
Key vocabulary	• position • arrange • the same • different • before • after • in between • pattern • standing up • lying down • shape names	• position • arrange • repeating pattern • the same • different • cube • cuboid • cone • arch	• position • arrangement • repeating pattern • cube • cuboid • sphere • cone • square-based pyramid
Opportunities for assessment	• selects blocks to create a sequence and copies this to make a pattern • can describe pattern made using appropriate mathematical language	• selects and names shapes to construct pattern • can describe type of pattern made (ABAB etc.) • can reproduce pattern accurately in a drawing	• can draw design showing repeating pattern • can follow design to construct pattern with bricks • uses mathematical language to talk about pattern and identify its type

Example 5.2   Shopping bags

Learning context: graphics area
Learning objectives:

- Talk about, recognize and recreate patterns (ELG)
- Describe patterns or relationships involving shapes (PNS Yl)
- Describe patterns and relationships involving shapes and make predictions (PNS Y2)

	FS	Y1	Y2
Activity	Children stick paper clothes silhouettes in a pattern and use joining materials to make a simple 'shopping bag'. Children embellish with own graphics.	Children draw clothes pattern and embellish with own graphics. Make into a simple 'shopping bag'.	As Y1.
Resources	Paper silhouettes of T-shirts, trousers, skirts; writing materials; paper of varying size and colour; sticky tape; hole punch; ribbon.	Writing and drawing materials; paper of varying size and colour; sticky tape; hole punch; ribbon.	As Y1.
Prompt and key questions	The clothes shop needs some new shopping bags. Can you design and make a shopping bag with a repeating clothes pattern on the front? What else can you write on the bag? What pattern have you made? What comes next/before/in between?	The clothes shop needs some new shopping bags. Can you design and make a shopping bag with a repeating clothes pattern on the front? What type of pattern have you made?	The clothes shop needs some new shopping bags. Can you design and make a shopping bag with different line patterns on the front? What is different about each of the patterns? Can you describe each pattern? How many times have you used the same shape in each pattern?
Key vocabulary	• the same • different • before • after • in between • shape names	• the same • different • before • after • in between • repeating pattern • shape names	• the same • different • repeating pattern • shape names
Opportunities for assessment	• selects paper clothes silhouettes to create sequence and copies this to make a pattern • can describe the pattern using appropriate mathematical language	• draws repeating pattern and is able to describe it using mathematical language • can identify the type of pattern they have made (ABBABB etc.)	• draws repeating patterns • can describe the type of patterns made • can discuss similarities and differences between the patterns with increasing use of mathematical language

Example 5.3   Price labels for charity clothes shop

Learning context: graphics area
Learning objectives:

- Talk about, recognize and recreate patterns (ELG)
- Describe patterns and relationships involving numbers; decide whether examples satisfy given conditions (PNS Y1)
- Describe patterns and relationships involving numbers, make predictions and test these with examples (PNS Y2)

	FS	Y1	Y2
Activity	Children design and make price tags for clothes shop. Use in clothes shop and develop related role play.	As FS.	As FS.
Resources	Card; scissors; hole punch; pieces of string; coloured pens/pencils; number line 0–10.	As FS, but include a price list: socks 2p, T-shirts 4p, shorts 6p ...	As FS, but include a price list: vests 10p, tights 20p, trousers 40p ...
Prompt and key questions	Can you design and make some price tags for the clothes shop? Start at 1p. Each price tag you write must be 1p more than the last one. What do you notice? Can you put them in order? Can you see a pattern in the numbers you have written? Can you talk about what you notice?	Look at the price list in the graphics area. Do you notice a pattern in the prices? Can you design and make some price tags for these values? Can you make more price tags, continuing the pattern you have spotted?	As Y1.
Key vocabulary	• number names • amount • getting bigger • more than • 1 more than	• amount • order • pattern • even numbers • increase • greater than	• amount • order • increase • pattern • doubles
Opportunities for assessment	• attempts to write numerals • writes numerals correctly • orders prices written correctly • makes links between values written and number line • can identify and talk about numbers increasing by 1	• writes prices correctly • can identify and talk about pattern on the price list • can continue the pattern accurately, calculating what comes next and why	• uses £.p notation correctly • can identify and talk about pattern on the price list • can continue the pattern accurately, calculating or predicting what comes next and why

Example 5.4   Mrs Mopple's breakfast

Learning context: role play
Learning objectives:

- Talk about, recognize and recreate patterns (ELG)
- Describe patterns and relationships involving numbers or shapes (PNS YI)
- Describe patterns or relationships involving numbers or shapes and make predictions (PNS Y2)

	FS	Y1	Y2
Activity	Children set out kitchen items in a pattern on the kitchen table. Develop kitchen and laundry role play.	As FS.	As FS.
Resources	Simple clothes airer; pegs; washing basket with washing; 'washing machine'; toy ironing board and iron; dressing up clothes; kitchen role-play resources (cups, plates, cutlery, etc.); large and small boxes of breakfast cereals; toy food; writing materials.	As FS.	As FS.
Prompt and key questions	Mrs Mopple is going to have breakfast before she begins the washing. She likes to put things out in repeating patterns in her kitchen. Can you put things on the kitchen table in a pattern? Can you describe the patterns you have made?	Mrs Mopple likes to put things in repeating patterns in her kitchen. Can you use the things in her kitchen to make as many different patterns as you can? Can you describe the patterns you made? How many different patterns did you make?	Mrs Mopple likes to put things in her kitchen in repeating patterns. She wants to find out how many different patterns she can make. Can you make a record for her of the patterns she makes? Can you record it as ABAB, AABB, etc.?
Key vocabulary	• the same • different • before • after • in between	• the same • different • change • repeating patterns	• the same • different • repeating patterns
Opportunities for assessment	• selects role-play resources to create a sequence and copies this to make a pattern • can describe pattern using appropriate mathematical language	• can construct a variety of different patterns using a variety of resources • can describe pattern using appropriate mathematical language	• can construct and describe a variety of patterns using different resources • can interpret and record patterns as ABAB etc.

Example 5.5   Button patterns

Learning context: play tray
Learning objectives:

- Talk about, recognize and recreate patterns (ELG)
- Describe patterns and relationships involving shapes (PNS Y1)
- Describe patterns and relationships involving shapes and make predictions (PNS Y2)

	FS	Y1	Y2
Activity	Children design button layout on clothes by selecting different buttons and laying them in a repeating pattern on clothes silhouettes.	As FS.	As FS.
Resources	Flat (cement-mixing) play tray; selection of buttons of different shapes, sizes, colours; large clothes silhouettes (card silhouettes of trousers, T-shirts, etc., covered in fabric).	As FS.	As FS.
Prompt and key questions	The clothes being made in the factory need to have buttons on them. Can you choose which buttons you would like to use and lay them in a pattern? What comes next/before/in between? Can you describe your pattern?	The clothes being made in the factory need to have buttons on them, but they must be in a repeating pattern. Can you make 1 pattern, then think about which type of button you could add or take away to change the pattern. Describe the patterns you have made. What types of pattern are they?	As Y1.
Key vocabulary	- shape names - colours - the same - different - before - after - in between - pattern	- shape names - change - the same - different - repeating pattern	- shape names - repeating pattern
Opportunities for assessment	- selects buttons to create a sequence and copies this to make a pattern - can describe pattern using appropriate mathematical language	- names shapes used to construct pattern - can describe type of pattern (ABAB etc.)	- names shapes used to construct pattern - can describe pattern with increasing use of mathematical language

Example 5.6   Mrs Mopple's patterns

Learning context: washing line
Learning objectives:

- Talk about, recognize and recreate patterns (ELG)
- Describe patterns and relationships involving numbers or shapes (PNS Y1)
- Describe patterns and relationships involving numbers or shapes, make predictions and test these with examples (PNS Y2)

	FS	Y1	Y2
Activity	Children hang socks and hankies in a repeating pattern. Develop role play based on Mrs Mopple.	Children investigate how many different patterns they can make with the washing and record pictorially. Develop role play based on Mrs Mopple.	As Y1, but children predict how many different patterns they will be able to make with the washing.
Resources	Washing line; pegs; washing basket; 6 socks; 6 hankies; toy ironing board with iron.	In addition to FS: clipboard and writing materials.	As Y1.
Prompt and key questions	Mrs Mopple likes to hang her washing out in a pattern. Can you help her by hanging out the washing in the basket in a pattern? Can you describe your pattern? What comes next/in between/before?	Mrs Mopple likes to hang her washing out in a pattern. Can you help her to find out how many different patterns she can make with this washing and make a record for her? What types of patterns have you made? How many different patterns have you made?	Mrs Mopple likes to hang her washing out in a pattern. Can you predict how many different patterns she could make with the washing? What can you do to find out? Can you record your results for Mrs Mopple? Were your predictions accurate?
Key vocabulary	• the same • different • next • before • in between	• the same • different • repeating patterns	• repeating patterns • prediction • result
Opportunities for assessment	• selects clothes to make simple sequence and repeats to make a pattern • describes pattern accurately	• constructs different patterns • can talk about patterns made and identify type of pattern (AABBAABB etc.) • can record patterns made pictorially	• tackles problem in a logical and organized way • makes sensible predictions • can record possible patterns • constructs a variety of patterns and describes what type of pattern they are

Photo 5.3 Using buttons to make repeating patterns.

 Creative ideas for good practice

- Model pattern making in the learning environment through the setting out of resources, use of displays and daily activities.
- Avoid teaching pattern as a 'unit of work', but instead highlight it in all daily activities and mathematical events as it occurs.
- Provide opportunities for children to see, hear and feel pattern through works of art, music and dance.
- Encourage children to both observe and create patterns in a variety of media.
- Encourage children to talk about the patterns they see and create, and to identify the types of pattern they are (whether ABAB, AABB, etc.).

Suggested further reading

Haylock, D. and Cockburn, A. (2008) *Understanding Mathematics for Young Children*, 3rd edition. London: Sage Publications.

Montague-Smith, A. (2002) *Mathematics in Nursery Education,* 2nd edition. London: David Fulton Publishers.

Pound, L. (1999) *Supporting Mathematical Development in the Early Years.* Buckingham: Open University Press.

Rhydderch- Evans, Z. (1993) *Mathematics in the School Grounds.* Devon: Southgate Publishers Ltd.

6

Shape and space

This chapter covers:

- concepts developed during activities using 3D and 2D shapes
- exploring shapes in the environment
- position and movement in play, and the use of ICT
- examples of focused teaching activities and recorded work, along with independent activities based on the theme of 'the street'.

Meaningful exploration of shapes is essential for good quality teaching and learning. When children construct a model for a specific purpose, for example, it is *their* experience and their understanding of the shapes' properties and the shapes' relationships with one another, that will inform the decisions and actions they take, not their knowledge of shape names. Children need to have a wide range of experiences with shapes, including:

- drawing around 2D and 3D shapes

- making pictures with 2D shapes

- making models with 3D shapes

- posting shapes through holes

- moving their bodies in and out of structures

- sculpting and decompressing shapes made with malleable materials

- discussing shapes with adults and peers.

These are the very experiences that act as the basis of geometrical analysis at a later stage (Haylock and Cockburn, 2003). It is crucial, therefore, that young children should be stimulated and excited enough to want to 'move shapes around' and have support from practitioners who can model mathematical vocabulary and encourage concept development.

3D shapes

When working with 3D shapes, children will be developing their understanding of:

- the relationship between the faces of a shape and its movement (does it roll or slide?)

- arrangements and packing (can the shape be stacked easily?)

- the shape's properties

- relationships between shapes.

Young children will have spent much of their formative lives engaging with 3D shapes and therefore may well be familiar with their properties, if not their mathematical names. Practitioners therefore need to build on the experiences young children have had with these shapes, and not overlook this in preference for relatively low quality name-learning activities, such as colouring in pictures of 3D shapes. Children need to manipulate shapes in a wide variety of materials and in different contexts, where mathematical vocabulary is sensitively introduced and modelled, and where children have real reasons to practise using it:

- **Block play**
  Both unit and large hollow blocks provide children with the experience of exploring the properties of shape within the context of imaginative play, pursuing their own schematic play and in problem solving (Gura, 1992). While the smaller unit blocks can be used to construct small worlds, the large hollow blocks can be used to create trains, boats, caves and an abundance of other imaginative settings.

- **Commercial construction kits**
  Although these kits are prescriptive in terms of possibilities, they allow children to explore a wide range of shapes to fit a specific purpose.

- **Recyclable materials and modelling dough**
  Children can assemble and disassemble, stretch and compress, giving them valuable experience at moving aspects of their model to change its function. Working with clay or modelling dough gives children the chance to create a 3D shape they may not yet have the skills to draw, and again allows them to explore how form and function can be changed in this malleable material.

2D shapes

Activities which will help children develop concepts of 2D shapes are:

- making pictures by combining 2D shapes (using shapes themselves, or by drawing around shapes)

- making patterns (see Chapter 5)

- exploring faces of 3D shapes, by manipulating the nets of shapes and printing with the faces

- exploring different thickness and orientation of lines through drawing, painting, sewing, collage

- observing and moving shapes, discovering that some shapes do not change their appearance when turned through certain angles (rotational symmetry), and that some shapes look exactly the same on each side when folded (line of symmetry).

 Principles into practice

Making pictures with 2D shapes (see Example 6.2 below) helps lay foundations for geometrical analysis. During these experiences, children will be:

- moving the same shape, without turning it, from one position to another (exploring translation)
- turning shapes (exploring rotation)
- observing that the two halves of some shapes are the same (becoming aware of line symmetry)
- noticing that the same shape can appear in different sizes (exploring scaling up or down by a factor)
- discovering how some shapes fit together well while others do not (exploring tessellation)
- noticing that there can be different types of squares and triangles (becoming aware of family likeness).

Shape in the environment

Our environment, both internal and external, is full of shapes which young children can observe and interact with. Young children and babies, as soon as they are physically able, handle, touch, smell and taste 3D shapes. Studying shapes in the environment provides excellent, imaginative links with geography, literacy and mathematics. Tables 6.1 and Table 6.2 on page 89 illustrate realistic links between two popular early years geography-based themes and maths and literacy. School grounds themselves offer an abundance of opportunities to explore shape and space through observing, drawing and replicating in a variety of media and model-making features such as buildings, brick patterns, stone, pathways, plants, leaves, fencing, etc.

Shape in art

Once again, works of art provide stimulus for the exploration of shape, both 2D and 3D work. Sharing works of art can stimulate the use of mathematical vocabulary and inspire children to create their own work using a variety of media in the style of a particular artist. Particularly useful pieces are by the following artists (see Resources):

- Piet Mondrian

- Andy Goldsworthy

- Auguste Herbin

- Barbara Hepworth.

- Wassily Kandinsky.

Table 6.1 Local environment

Geography/Knowledge and understanding of the world	Opportunities for exploring shape and space	Links with literacy
• Carry out fieldwork – go for a shape walk, observing brick/stone work in paths, fencing, buildings, etc.	• Create drawings and collages of patterns and shapes observed.	• *The Big Concrete Lorry* (and other Trotter Street stories) by Shirley Hughes.
• Collect natural materials – leaves, twigs, flowers, shells, pebbles, etc.	• Provide a play tray containing natural materials, magnifying lens and sketching materials. Children observe, sort, sketch materials.	• *Snail Trail* by Ruth Brown.
• Discuss route from home to school. • Carry out a vehicle survey.	• Explore pictorial map making and use of simple coordinates. • Use construction kits and wooden blocks to build a variety of vehicles.	• *Traffic Jam* by Annie Owen. • Develop traffic role play.
• Create small world scene of local environment. Use geographical language and simple coordinates.	• Use reclaimed materials to construct axels. • Give directions, follow road signs, construct parking bays. • Use positional language and simple coordinates.	• Develop narrative for small world play.

Table 6.2 Islands and seasides

Geography/Knowledge and understanding of the world	Opportunities for exploring shape and space	Links with literacy
• Make picture maps of real and imaginary island and seaside scenes. Use appropriate geographical language: island, coastline, hill, dune, sea, ocean, etc.	• Try map making, drawing and positioning shapes. Use positional and spatial language.	• *Come Away From the Water, Shirley* by John Burningham.
• Set up small world drama/role play using toy and real seaside artefacts.	• Use spatial and positional language.	• *Jack's Fantastic Voyage* by Michael Foreman.
• Carry out fieldwork and collect beach artefacts.	• Provide a play tray filled with beach artefacts for sorting/drawing/imaginary play.	• *Katie Morag and the Two Grandmothers* (and other Katie Morag stories) by Mairi Hedderwick.
	• Create observational drawings and paintings, sculpture and fabric and thread.	• Develop narrative in voyage/ferry boat/pirate role play.

Position and movement

Activities in which children move artefacts from one point to the next and draw representations of the resultant image will enable them to develop concepts of position (including observing features from different positions), direction and distance. There is huge scope for this type of activity in the early years classroom (some of which are detailed in the Examples below). We can begin by considering the main categories of experience.

Small worlds

As seen in Chapter 2, these offer excellent opportunities for linking geography and mathematics. By providing resources that children can manipulate to create roads, enclosures, pathways, bridges, tunnels, oceans, rivers, parking spaces, etc., children can extend their understanding of concepts of shape and space to create small worlds that fit their purpose. Teaching and learning using small worlds can be developed by:

- introducing characters or vehicles that can be moved around the scene in order to give children a purpose for developing a narrative in which positional language is used

- varying the place in which small worlds are set up, sometimes on table-tops (allowing the children a good view down onto the scene) and sometimes on the floor (allowing children both to sit around it and to 'get into' the scene)

- involving children in the setting up of a small world, either by following a simple plan or in the retelling of a story or route

- encouraging different children to describe what they see as they sit around a small world. A feature near to one child will be far away from the child sitting opposite, for example, thus enabling them to compare their perspectives and to discuss why their views differ

- encouraging children to draw picture maps of what they see and compare them with those of their peers. Some children have a very keen sense of shape and space and can represent the position and orientation of features very accurately

- by throwing ribbon over the small world scene and using letter and numeral cards to create simple coordinates which can be used to describe the precise location of a specific feature.

ICT
Concepts of shape and space can be imaginatively and creatively explored by using various forms of ICT.

Digital camera

Digital cameras can be used to take photographs of small world scenes from different positions. This is an instant way of illustrating how views from different positions can vary. Photos taken of features of the school grounds, visited locations and journeys en route can be used to stimulate the use of positional language and vocabulary used to describe shapes. This is particularly useful when using photos as a slideshow or to recreate a visited location in small world play.

Programmable robots

Directional language and movement can be explored creatively by using programmable robots such as Roamer™, Bee-bot or PIXIE (see Resources). Layouts can be made from large sheets of paper or card that depict scenes from stories or other specific locations. Drawing a grid on the layout enables children to estimate more easily how far the robot needs to travel in order to reach a particular destination. Children can then program the equipment to follow set routes and give instructions to partners. The robots can be 'dressed' to become a character or vehicle in order to make their use more meaningful. Some of these robots, such as PIXIE, are useful in exploring whole, half, quarter turns and direction (see Table 8.4).

Interactive whiteboard

Although this resource is unsuitable for most independent activity, it is very valuable for direct teaching in class and group work. Interactive whiteboard (IWB) files can be made using images related to the children's interests, or current theme, which can be manipulated to create a meaningful context. Examples include:

- playing the 'pack the picnic' game where 'food' (either images of real food packaging or regular 2D shapes) can be rotated to fit into the picnic basket, thus encouraging the use of positional language

- hiding 2D shapes behind an image of a theme-related object or character, gradually revealing it to encourage talk describing and identifying features, and predicting shapes

- using a slideshow of photos of environmental features or works of art to identify 2D shapes or repeating patterns within them

- moving and exploring lines of different length to join, form shapes or make routes

- sorting 2D shapes into 'bags' or 'boxes' using agreed criteria

- creating repeating patterns with regular 2D shapes using the IWB grouping and cloning tools

- using Numicon® software, enabling images of the Numicon plates to be rotated to fit together and therefore be seen much more clearly than the plates themselves in a class situation.

Photo 6.1   Programming PIXIE, dressed as a frog, to explore a route across the 'pond'.

Commercial software is available for route exploration using the IWB. Roamer™ and RoamerWorld, its related software, are useful resources for encouraging positional and directional language, and the use of the IWB allows the activity to be seen clearly and effectively in class situations.

Sculpture and model making

Making sculptures and models using a variety of materials provides children with opportunities to move objects, experiment with positions and use positional language when they discuss their work. Youngsters may be:

- making sculptures on a black cloth on a table or in a cement-mixing tray using a variety of natural and manufactured materials (see Chapter 2)

- using wooden blocks laid out in specific arrangements (circles, spirals, curved or zigzag walls)

- modelling using recyclable materials to cut, disassemble and join

- using clay or modelling dough.

PE

The potential of PE activities in helping to develop a sense of space, position and, importantly, a movement vocabulary should not be underestimated. When children use large apparatus, they will be moving over, under, through, inside, in between and along pathways that might be curved or zigzagged. Dance offers many opportunities for children to hear, interpret and use movement and positional language. Inviting children to move with a variety of props can act to stimulate their own movement and descriptive language. Typical props might be:

- long ribbons

- silk scarves

- plastic mirrors/sheets of reflective paper

- balloons/balls

- bubbles.

Introducing descriptive vocabulary, commenting positively on a child's movement, and encouraging children to describe the movement of others, all facilitate the use of this mathematical vocabulary in a creative and meaningful way (Tucker, 2002b).

Positional vocabulary

Under, inside, outside, beside, in between, through, towards, next to, left, right, near, far away from, forwards, backwards, sideways, across, direction, turn, half a turn, a quarter turn.

Examples of activities

Activity 6.1   Shopping Bag

Learning objective:	Exploring features and properties of 3D shapes.
Resources:	Shopping bag containing everyday 3D packaging; plain paper; paint.
How to begin:	Ask the children to unpack the shopping bag and find ways to stack the packages, encouraging them to talk about which shapes will/will not roll as they do so. Use this activity as a means of encouraging the children to discuss the properties of the shapes they are handling. As the children to talk about the shape of the items' faces, ask the children to select a particular item, paint each face and print with it on the same large piece of paper.
Development:	Ask the children to describe the prints they have made and encourage other children to identify which package made these prints and ask them to explain their reasoning.
Key vocabulary:	Roll; slide; curved; straight; cube; cuboid; cylinder; round; square; oblong; circle.
Extension:	Using the IWB, display each face of a 3D shape. Encourage the children to discuss what they see and, using their observations and deductions, suggest which shape it might be.

Activity 6.2   Shadow Puppets

Learning objective: Exploring features and properties of 2D shapes.

Resources: Assorted 2D shapes in black sugar paper; art straws; glue; sticky tape.

How to begin: Invite the children to use the shapes to make simple vehicles, building and street sign shapes that can be used to create a shadow puppet play set in the street. Allow the children time to explore the shapes before selecting which ones they would like to stick together to create their person, vehicle or building. This activity provides opportunities for children to explore the properties of shapes, tessellation and a context for the use of shape vocabulary and mathematical names.

Development: Once the puppets are made, they should be attached to dowelling. Then, using a large sheet of white cotton as a screen with a projector, or other light source, positioned behind it, the children can develop their play. Use the experience to generate mathematical talk about which shapes were the most popular in the puppet making, which worked best and why.

Key vocabulary: Curved; straight; round; big; small; square; oblong; circle; semicircle; triangle.

Activity 6.3   Delivery Van Directions

Learning objectives: Exploring and developing the language of position, direction and movement.

Resources: Wooden unit blocks/hollow wooden blocks/building crates; toy delivery van.

How to begin: This activity lends itself to the indoor environment on a small scale, or outdoors using big construction apparatus and a ride-on 'delivery van'. Ask the children to use the construction equipment to make a layout of streets, creating a simple network of roads the 'delivery van' can drive through. Encourage the children to think of particular shops or buildings they would like to feature and these can be labelled. The children can take it in turns to make deliveries to specific shops by following the instructions given by their friends. Encourage the use of key vocabulary.

Development: Introduce into the scene a small programmable robot such as PIXIE (see Resources). This can be covered with a card 'jacket' to make it more like a delivery van. Allow the children time to explore PIXIE, then working in pairs, one child gives instructions to a destination of his or her choice, while the other child programs PIXIE accordingly. This provides many opportunities to use vocabulary of space and also to estimate distances the robot will have to travel.

Key vocabulary: Forwards; backwards; sideways; near; far; turn; right; left.

Emily was able to give and follow instructions on her delivery van. She is beginning to use left and right accurately.

Photo 6.2

Activity 6.4   The Bus Journey

Learning objective: Exploring features and properties of 2D and 3D shapes.

Resources: Assorted large wooden blocks or plastic crates; dressing up clothes; card; writing materials.

(Continued)

(Continued)

How to begin:	Ask the children to select the wooden blocks or crates to construct a 'bus' so they can travel into town. Encourage the children to talk about which shapes to select and which shapes fit together well. Use this opportunity to model key vocabulary and encourage the children to use it in their mathematical talk. Encourage the children to make sure there are enough seats for each of them.
Development:	Once the bus is constructed, the children might like to make bus tickets and road signs using card and writing materials. Again, this provides opportunities for the children to practise using mathematical language to describe and name 2D shapes, and to explore their properties in a meaningful context. Encourage the children to develop bus journey role play, heightening the profile of the key vocabulary.
Key vocabulary:	Long; short; fits together; flat sides; faces; square; oblong; cube; cuboid.
Extension:	This activity, of course, also lends itself to developing many other mathematical areas, such as:

- estimation and measurement – How long/wide will the bus have to be? Is the bus long enough/wide enough for all of the passengers? How can we measure it?
- counting and calculation – Have we got enough seats for all of the passengers? How can we find out? How many more do we need to make?
- money and calculation – How much does your ticket cost? How can you make that amount? Will you need some change?

As the activity draws on all of these areas, it is advisable for the practitioner to select a main focus for the activity on which to concentrate, but ensuring the other areas are addressed to make the mathematics 'real'.

 Principles into practice

- Avoid over-emphasis on name learning, ensuring that children are involved in activities where they are experiencing and discussing the properties of shapes.
- Provide opportunities for children to sculpt shapes with malleable materials, changing them by stretching and compression.
- Explore ways to make links with aspects of the geography and KUW to give real purpose for developing positional language and spatial awareness.
- Avoid over-use of commercial regular 2D and 3D shapes, and use 2D and 3D works of art to stimulate the use of mathematical vocabulary, and creative picture and model making.

Examples of independent activities: The street

Example 6.1   Prints in modelling dough

Learning context: malleable materials
Learning objectives:

- Use language such as 'circle' or 'bigger' to describe the shape and size of solids and flat shapes (ELG)
- Visualize and name common 2D shapes and 3D solids and describe their features (PNS YI)
- Visualize common 2D shapes and 3D solids and identify shapes from pictures of them, referring to their properties (PNS Y2)

	FS	Y1	Y2
Activity	Children use a selection of items from a 'shopping bag' to print in modelling dough. Children discuss the shape of the prints made and use them to make their own patterns.	As FS.	In addition to FS, children work with a partner who tries to identify the shape whose face has made the print.
Resources	A 'shopping bag' that contains a selection of pasta shapes, cylindrical battery, empty aerosol can, small cuboid and cube packaging; modelling dough.	As FS.	As FS.
Prompt and key questions	Look at the shopping in the bag. What prints do you think they will make in the modelling dough? How are the prints they make different from each other? Can you tell which object made which print? How did you work that out?	As FS.	Look at the items of shopping from the bag. Can you think what shapes their faces will make in the modelling dough? Make some prints and ask a friend to work out which of the items made the print and why.
Key vocabulary	<ul><li>straight</li><li>curved</li><li>round</li><li>wavy</li><li>stretch</li><li>bend</li><li>circle</li><li>square</li><li>oblong</li></ul>	<ul><li>straight</li><li>curved</li><li>circle</li><li>oblong</li><li>square</li><li>cylinder</li><li>cube</li><li>cuboid</li></ul>	<ul><li>straight</li><li>curved</li><li>circle</li><li>oblong</li><li>cube</li><li>cuboid</li><li>regular</li><li>irregular</li></ul>
Opportunities for assessment	<ul><li>can use shape vocabulary to describe properties</li><li>uses vocabulary of shape and position to describe prints</li><li>can name and identify some simple 2D and 3D shapes</li></ul>	<ul><li>can use increasing range of vocabulary to describe shape properties</li><li>uses vocabulary of shape and position to describe prints</li><li>can name and identify some 2D and 3D shapes</li></ul>	<ul><li>can use increasing range of vocabulary to describe shape properties</li><li>uses vocabulary of shape and position to describe prints</li><li>can name and identify an increasing range of 2D and 3D shapes</li></ul>

Example 6.2   Kandinsky houses

Learning context: table-top
Learning objectives:

- Use language such as 'circle' or 'bigger' to describe the shape and size of flat shapes (ELG)
- Visualize and name common 2D shapes and use them to make pictures (PNS YI)
- Sort, make and describe 2D shapes, referring to their properties (PNS Y2)

	FS	Y1	Y2
Activity	Children look at and discuss a selection of prints by Kandinsky (or Herbin), using this to inspire making their own pictures with coloured 2D shapes. Children talk about and describe their pictures.	As FS.	As FS.
Resources	A selection of prints by Kandinsky or Herbin; table covered in black velvet cloth; white cardboard picture frames; assorted coloured 2D shapes.	As FS.	As FS.
Prompt and key questions	Look at the Kandinsky prints and notice the different shapes and colours he uses. What ideas does it give you? Can you use these ideas to make your own picture of a street scene? Can you describe your picture? What shapes have you used and why? Which shapes fit together and which do not?	As FS.	As FS.
Key vocabulary	• curved • straight • round • circle • bigger than • smaller than • fits together • shape names	• curved • straight • square • oblong • triangle • circle • semi circle • fits together	• area • curved • straight • tessellation • circle • semi-circle • square • oblong • pentagon • hexagon
Opportunities for assessment	• can use vocabulary of shape and position to describe picture • can observe and discuss similarities and differences between shapes • can identify and name simple 2D shapes	• can use vocabulary of shape and position to describe picture • can observe and discuss similarities and differences between a variety of simple 2D shapes • can identify and name an increasing range of simple 2D shapes	• can use increasing a range of mathematical language to describe picture • can identify, name and talk about the properties of an increasing range of 2D shapes

Photo 6.3 This child uses 2D shapes to create her own picture inside a white card frame in response to discussion about the work of Kandinsky and Herbin.

Example 6.3   View from a hot-air balloon

Learning context: small world drama
Learning objectives:

- Use everyday words to describe position (ELG)
- Use everyday language to describe the position of objects and direction and distance when moving them (PNS YI)
- Follow and give instructions involving position, direction and movement (PNS Y2)

	FS	Y1	Y2
Activity	• Children engage with small world drama of town scene, countryside and coastline. Children develop narrative of travellers in the hot-air balloon, describing what they can see below as they fly over the scene.	As FS.	As FS.
Resources	• Green, brown, blue drapes; small wooden houses/buildings; assorted vehicles and road signs; play people; a selection of farm animals; stones, bark, twigs (to construct animal enclosures); boats; sea animals; hot-air balloon (made from papier mache over a balloon, and yoghurt pot suspended from it).	As FS.	As FS, but also clipboard and writing materials.
Prompt and key questions	• The travellers are flying over a town. Can you be a traveller and describe what you see to your companion? What lies below you? What is in front/ behind you? What is nearest to you/ further away?	As FS.	The travellers are travelling over the town. They need to find the most interesting route over the countryside, and town and to the coast. Talk to your companion about the most interesting route and write or draw instructions for other travellers to follow.
Key vocabulary	• on top • underneath • beside • near • far • next to • turn	• underneath • above • near • turn • opposite • right • left • between • middle	• underneath • below • opposite • turn • right • left • between • middle
Opportunities for assessment	• can use positional language to describe journey	• can use positional language with increasing accuracy to describe journey	• can use positional language with increasing accuracy to describe journey • can represent small world scene accurately in a drawing

Example 6.4   Symmetrical shapes

Learning context: play tray
Learning objectives:

- Use everyday words to describe position (ELG)
- Identify shapes that turn about a point or line (PNS YI)
- Identify reflective symmetry in patterns and 2D shapes (PNS Y2)

	FS	Y1	Y2
Activity	Children explore line symmetry by holding mirrors alongside a selection of half pictures. They explore moving the mirror across the pictures in different ways until the reflection completes the image. Children discuss the shapes and images they see.	As FS, but children also make their own symmetrical drawings to investigate with the mirror.	As Y1.
Resources	6 half pictures; 2 small, flat plastic mirrors.	In addition to FS: paper and drawing materials.	As Y1.
Prompt and key questions	How do the pictures change when you hold the mirror against them? Can you describe what you see? As you move the mirror over the picture, where is the mirror when the picture and reflection make the whole shape? What do you notice?	In addition to FS: Can you make your own symmetrical drawing? What happens when you hold the mirror alongside?	As YI.
Key vocabulary	• longer • shorter • reflection • the same • whole • complete • upwards • downwards • turn	• the same • reflection • symmetrical	• reflection • symmetrical • line of symmetry
Opportunities for assessment	• uses mathematical vocabulary to describe activity • recognizes and identifies when reflection creates whole picture	• uses mathematical vocabulary to describe activity • can identify symmetrical nature of the pictures • can create own simple symmetrical picture	• can recognize and identify symmetrical nature of the pictures • uses vocabulary of symmetry and reflection • can create own simple symmetrical picture

Example 6.5   Sorting parcels

Learning context: role play
Learning objectives:

- Use language such as 'circle' or 'bigger' to describe the shape and size of solids and flat shapes (ELG)
- Visualize and name common 3D solids and describe their features (PNS YI)
- Identify 3D solids, form pictures of them in different positions and sort and describe, referring to their properties (PNS Y2)

	FS	Y1	Y2
Activity	Children discuss and sort a variety of parcels into labelled sacks. Children develop Post Office role play.	As FS.	As FS, but children also record how many of each shape of parcel have been sorted.
Resources	Assorted, wrapped parcels including cubes, cuboids and cylinders; 3 large sacks each labelled with picture and corresponding shape name: , 'cube' 'cuboid' and 'cylinder'; writing materials; typical dressing-up clothes and Post Office resources.	As FS.	As FS.
Prompt and key questions	The Post Office workers need to sort the parcels into sacks. Can you look carefully at the shapes of the parcels and find ways to sort them into the sacks. How have you sorted the parcels? What is the same/different about the parcels? Which shapes have flat/curved faces? Which shapes roll? Why?	The Post Office workers need to sort the parcels into sacks. Look carefully at the labels on the sacks and sort the parcels into the correct sacks. Can you describe the parcels you need to a friend? What are the differences and similarities between the shapes? Which shapes have flat/curved faces? Which shapes roll? Why?	The Post Office workers need to sort the parcels into sacks and make a record of how many of each shape of parcel they have sorted. Can you sort the parcels into the correct sack and find a way of keeping a record for the manager when the Post Office closes? What information does your record give us about the parcels?
Key vocabulary	• straight • curved • edge • face • roll • slide • square	• straight • curved • circle • oblong • cube • cuboid • cylinder	• circle • oblong • cube • cuboid • cylinder
Opportunities for assessment	• uses shape vocabulary to describe properties • selects, uses and explains criteria used to sort parcels • identifies and names some 2D and 3D shapes	• uses shape vocabulary to describe properties • can relate solid shapes to pictures of them • identifies and names some 2D and 3D shapes	• can relate solid shapes to pictures of them • identifies and names cube, cuboid and cylinder • designs simple means of recording numbers of parcels sorted and can talk about the information it shows

Example 6.6   Silhouette street

Learning context: play tray
Learning objectives:

- Use language such as 'circle' or 'bigger' to describe the shape and size of flat shapes (ELG)
- Visualize and name common 2D shapes and describe their features (PNS Y1)
- Make and describe 2D shapes, referring to their properties (PNS Y2)

	FS	Y1	Y2
Activity	Children select an envelope from the play tray and hold it up to a light source. They describe and identify the silhouette they see. Children develop a narrative around the silhouettes they see and describe the 'journey' they take down the street.	As FS.	As Y1, with increasing use of mathematical vocabulary.
Resources	6 sealed envelopes each containing a black sugar paper silhouette of a building with differently shaped cut-out windows.	As FS.	In addition to FS: clipboard and writing materials.

	FS	Y1	Y2
Prompt and key questions	These letters have been posted without an address. You can find out which building they are going to by holding them up to the light. Can you describe the buildings you see? Are the windows the same? What is the same/different about them? Which shapes are curved and which are straight?	As FS.	Can you describe the buildings in order to a friend? Can your friend draw them accurately following your description? Can you make up a story about travelling along this route?
Key vocabulary	• big • small • straight • curved • number names • square • circle • triangle • oblong	• straight • curved • square • oblong • circle • triangle • semi-circle • hexagon • pentagon	• square • oblong • triangle • circle • semi-circle • hexagon • pentagon • area • perimeter
Opportunities for assessment	• uses shape vocabulary to describe building silhouettes • identifies and names a variety of 2D shapes	• uses shape vocabulary to describe building silhouettes • identifies and accurately names a variety of 2D shapes	• uses shape vocabulary to describe building silhouettes accurately • can name and discuss the properties of an increasing number of 2D shapes

Suggested further reading 📖

Blinko, J. (2000) *Space, Shape and Measures*. London: A and C Black.

Elston, C. (2007) *Using ICT in the Primary School*. London: David Fulton Publishers.

English, R. (2006) *Mathematics and ICT in the Primary School: A Creative Approach*. London: David Fulton Publishers.

Haylock, D. and Cockburn, A. (2008) *Understanding Mathematics for Young Children*, 3rd edition. London: Sage Publications.

Linfield, R. S. and Coltman, P. (1999) *Planning and Learning through Shapes*. Leamington Spa: Step Forward Publishing.

Parton, G. (2000) *ICT: Early Years Activities to Promote the Use of Information and Communication Technology*. Dunstable: Belair Publications.

Rhydderch-Evans, Z. (1993) *Mathematics in the School Grounds*. Devon: Southgate Publishers.

Siraj-Blatchford, J. and Whitebread, D. (2003) *Supporting Information and Communication Technology in the Early Years*. London: Open University Press.

7

Measurement

> **This chapter covers:**
>
> - the progression of developing skills and concepts in measuring length
> - the terms 'weight' and 'mass'
> - imaginative ideas for measuring volume and capacity
> - exploring area and perimeter in play
> - using time in a playful context
> - examples of focused teaching activities and recorded work, along with independent activities based on the theme of 'pets'.

Arguably, measurement in all its forms is the aspect of mathematics that children have had most experience of prior to starting school. In their play and daily activities, children are continually estimating and making comparisons of weight, length, area, time and capacity. They will fill a cup with liquid, find a space big enough to lay out a road mat, mix powder paint to make a specific colour, all of which involve estimating and comparing amounts for the purpose of solving a problem. As children's skills and understanding of concepts develop, measuring will increasingly involve counting accurately, number operations and selecting and using appropriate measuring equipment. Practitioners need to ensure that the learning environment offers many opportunities for creative and spontaneous uses of measuring, which are supported and consolidated by focused teaching activities. Much of the volume and capacity work that is conducted in Key Stage 1 classrooms, for example, involves pouring sand and water when it is in fact possible to use a wide range of other materials that might hold more interest and relevance for young children (see Chapter 2), such as harvesting and cooking fruit and vegetables grown at the setting, or using resources related to a theme or book.

> **Creative ideas for good practice**
>
> *Rosie's Walk* by Pat Hutchins provides many opportunities for measurement in a small world layout of the story:
>
> - finding the distance Rosie travels from one feature to the next (length)
> - counting the number of toy sheep it would take to cover a field, or the number of toy ducks needed to cover the pond (area)
>
> *(Continued)*

(Continued)

- measuring the length of fencing required to go around the farmyard (perimeter)
- using a sand timer to find the time taken for PIXIE to travel around a specific route (time)

and in a play tray:

- using a sand timer to find the time taken to fill a small hessian sack with corn (time and capacity)
- finding the heaviest and lightest bags of corn/flour (weight).

It must be recognized that no measurement is 100% accurate, no matter what type of measurement is being undertaken or what measuring equipment is being used. All measurements involve a degree of rounding up or down. This provides a useful discussion point with older Key Stage 1 children.

When engaged in activities exploring length, weight, volume and capacity from the Foundation Stage through Key Stage 1, children will be developing the following skills and concepts:

- descriptive language

- measuring by comparison and using related language

- ordering objects by quantity

- counting accurately

- using and applying number operations

- using place value

- selecting and using appropriate measuring equipment.

Length

Children have much experience of measuring and estimating length in their play, such as finding blankets, toy fencing, construction pieces, dolls clothes, and painting/sculpting lines that are long or short enough to fit their purpose. Children's conceptual development of measuring length often develops by:

- comparison, discovering that the two ends of the wooden blocks they are comparing need to be held together in order to measure with any degree of accuracy

- selecting non-standard units, such as books, pencils, blocks, number lines, etc., laying them end to end and counting how many items they have used. This is a very valuable stage owing to the assessment opportunities it gives, and the valuable mathematical discussion it generates

- selecting a uniform non-standard unit such as same-sized bricks

- using a standard unit.

 Creative ideas for good practice

Using a small world floor layout of *Rosie's Walk* for a mixed age group class:

- Ask some children to measure the distance Rosie travels on her journey from the haycock to the beehive by filling in the space with selected non-standard units. Some children may notice that results depend on the length of the item chosen, contributing to the realization of the need for a uniform unit.
- Ask some children to suggest a uniform unit they can use to measure the distance such as same-sized wooden bricks, Unifix® cubes and so on. This useful intermediate stage, avoiding going straight to centimetres, provides children with measuring equipment they can easily handle and further opportunities to realize the need for a standard unit. If everyone chooses a different set of bricks to measure with, the results will not be the same and this heightens awareness of the need for standard units.
- Ask some children to measure the distance using standard units, selecting unit and measuring equipment appropriately.

Weight

In their play, children will determine the heaviest item by holding and comparing objects and need opportunities to develop appropriate vocabulary such as: heavy, heaviest, heavier than; light, lightest and lighter than. Important points to consider when teaching are:

- Children should be encouraged to describe their findings in complete sentences and, importantly, to say the reciprocal, such as 'The blue bag of treasure is heavier than the red bag. The red bag is lighter than the blue bag'.

- It can be difficult to make true comparisons of weight using a flat hand, so it is beneficial to have objects or materials in bags for the children to hold and compare. For focused teaching activities, the practitioner can have pre-prepared bags (filled with any suitable material) in the guise of theme-related items.

- Weight and mass are two distinct measurements. When children are finding out which object is heaviest by comparison with another object, they are determining the weight of the object, but when they are measuring using another object as a counterbalance, in a bucket balance for example, they are in fact determining the mass of the object.

- The mass of a specific object can be determined using a bucket balance by:
    - finding other objects that counterbalance
    - using uniform non-standard units such as Unifix® cubes to counterbalance
    - progressing to gram masses to counterbalance and provide a standard unit of measurement.

In their chapter on measures, Haylock and Cockburn (2003) suggest three important points for practitioners to consider, which are summarized as follows:

- Practitioners should be consistent with their use of language, referring to counterbalances used as masses, and not weights.

- Young children's weighing activities should mainly involve the use of balance-type apparatus.

- Practitioners should model and encourage the children to use the language 'weighs the same as' when the word weigh is used, for example 'The sack of corn weighs the same as 20 g' or 'The sack of corn has a mass of 20 g'. This acts to emphasize the equivalence that has emerged.

As well as focused teaching sessions, children should have available to them bucket balances and a variety of resources to use as counterbalances in their play. These should be particularly relevant to role play, both indoors and outdoors (see Chapter 2).

 Creative ideas for good practice

- Bags of 'treasure' (velvet bags tied with ribbon).
- Bags of 'corn', 'flour', 'porridge', 'oats' (small tied hessian sacks).
- Bags of 'potting compost', 'cement', 'sand' (small, thick, plastic sacks, thoroughly taped, with a handle).

Area and perimeter

These aspects of measurement are not commonly explored in early years education, but are often a feature of children's play. Children are accustomed to finding out how many things can cover a space, or surround a designated area. For example, in small world play, children might ask:

- how many cars will fill the car park space?

- how many buildings will fill the building plot?

- how will the railway layout need to go to fit on the table?

- how many pieces of fencing are needed to go around the pond?

In role play and in the outside play area, they might consider:

- how many people can sit on the mat?

- which sheet covers the cot mattress?

- how many wooden blocks are needed to build a wall around the house?

- how many books cover the surface of the table?

- how many plates cover the tablecloth?

- how many children can stand around the circle?

Practitioners should use the vocabulary of area and perimeter with children during their play and in focused teaching activities when the opportunity arises.

 Creative ideas for good practice

Children can explore the relationship between constant perimeter and changing area by:

- making enclosures for small world animals with thick string, discovering that although the length of string remains the same, the enclosure will hold a different number of sheep depending on how it is arranged
- making parking areas in the outside play area with blocks, discovering that 10 wooden blocks, for example, can be arranged in different ways to make parking spaces that hold different numbers of vehicles.

Volume and capacity

Volume is the 3D space an object occupies, while capacity is the amount a container holds. Much of the capacity work undertaken by children in early years settings involves the pouring of sand and water into different sorts of containers. As seen in Chapter 2, there are a variety of other materials that can be poured successfully. Adding colour to water and providing unusual containers can make capacity work more exciting for children, and help make it more relevant to their interests.

 Creative ideas for good practice

- Pouring 'milk' – white water (a small amount of white powder paint).
- Making 'jelly' – water with red food colour; jelly moulds of differing shapes and sizes; jug.
- Pouring pirates' 'grog' – brown water (a small amount of brown powder paint); jugs and 'tankards' (either real or plastic beakers covered in tin foil).
- Making a swamp – green food dye added to water; flour; jugs and bottles of graduated sizes.
- Making 'gloop cake' – corn flour; water; food colour; jugs and graduated cake tins.
- Pouring 'magic potion' – food colour; soap flakes (to give a pearlized effect); glitter; using jugs and interestingly shaped bottles (bubble bath, shampoo bottles, etc.).

Volume can be explored through model making using commercial construction kits, wooden blocks and recycled materials. 'Parcel sets' can be made by practitioners (by collecting interesting shaped packaging and covering in bright durable paper) and used in relation to themes or stories where presents are exchanged.

Time

When children are working with time, they will:

- use mathematical and historical language (before; next; after; tomorrow; yesterday; last week; next week; etc.)

- sequence events

- compare different units of time

- count

- use number operations

- select and use appropriate measuring equipment.

Children will be aware of time in their everyday experiences: the length of time from one birthday to the next, who is older or younger, the changes in a younger sibling, etc. They may also be involved in different activities on different days and notice changes in their environment with the passing of the seasons. As young children are so often concerned with the present, practitioners should encourage them to be aware of the order of the events in the learning environment by:

- using a visual timetable (displaying agreed symbols to represent events and activities during the day)

- encouraging children to sequence activities, such as cooking or model making, in the form of a simple flow diagram

- sequencing the events in a story or rhyme

- drawing attention (when appropriate) to the shape of the clock hands at specific times of the day: snack time, lunchtime, home time, etc.

Providing equipment for measuring time in role play enables children to practise skills by:

- writing down times/using clock faces to show the opening/closing times of a shop

- measuring the time a washing cycle takes in the launderette

- using a calendar to book holidays/doctor/hair appointments

- writing times on departure tickets

- recording times in log/appointment books.

In a mixed Foundation Stage and Key Stage 1 class, it is particularly important to ensure there is a clear progression of equipment available for children to select and use independently, ensuring that time rockers, sand timers, clocks and stop watches are on hand so that children can select equipment that matches their level of skill, understanding and appropriateness to the task. Children should also be encouraged to measure time intervals and not just read the time.

Examples of activities

 ### Activity 7.1   The Vet's Day

Learning objective: Use and understanding of the vocabulary of time.

Resources: Writing materials; analogue clock face (or pictures of the given times); A4 sheets for the appointment book; vet role-play resources.

How to begin: Following discussion about vets' work and related role play, discuss with the children the sorts of activities the vet might undertake during the day, using opportunities to introduce key vocabulary. Ask the children to draw pictures of the vet involved in various activities during the day. Encourage the children to discuss the events and the time of day they might occur, prompting the use of key vocabulary.

Development: Ask the children to sequence the pictures, describing when in the day they might occur.

Key vocabulary: First; before; next; after; later; last; then; morning; afternoon; o'clock and half past times.

Extension: Ask the children to complete pages in the 'appointment' book, to write down some appointments timed to o'clock or half past times, and write down, or draw, the nature of the appointment. Use this to stimulate further role play.

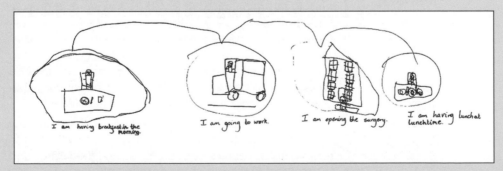

Figure 7.1   Nadine (R) can sequence familiar events

(Continued)

(Continued)

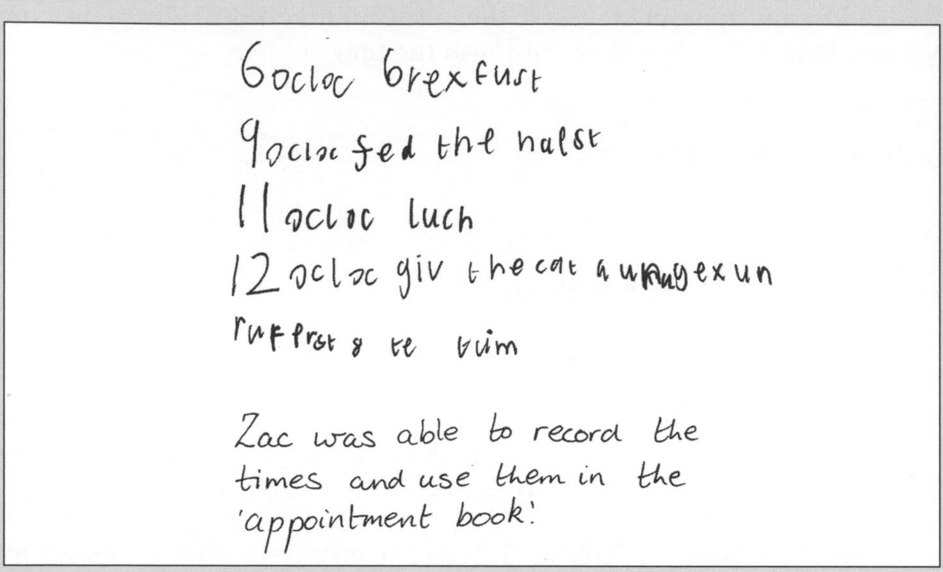

> 6ocloc brexfust
> 9ocloc fed the halst
> 11ocloc luch
> 12ocloc giv the cat a wurmgexun
> ruffrst g te vim
>
> Zac was able to record the
> times and use them in the
> 'appointment book'

Figure 7.2   Zac (Y2) can use and record time

Activity 7.2   Animal Blanket

Learning objective:	Heightening of awareness of the need for a uniform unit.
Resources:	Basket of same-sized and differently sized soft toys; small same-sized hand towel for each child.
How to begin:	Explain that the vet has some new blankets for the animals to sit on and they need to find out how many animals can sit on each blanket. Encourage the children to discuss how they might calculate this using the soft toys. This provides the opportunity for the children to cover their 'blanket' in soft toys selected from the basket. Ask the children to count how many toys cover the whole of the blanket, using this opportunity to introduce key words. Compare results and encourage a discussion about why some children will have different results even though their 'blankets' are identical in size. This activity not only allows children to compare and discuss size and area, but also helps to heighten their awareness of the importance of units chosen in determining an accurate and reliable result.
Development:	Following discussion, ask the children to find out how many animals they will need to cover the 'blanket' if the same-sized animals are used, again modelling and encouraging the use of key vocabulary.
Key vocabulary:	Cover; space; area; all over; more than; less than; equal numbers; number names.
Extension:	Children calculate the area accurately using uniform bricks, envelopes, Numicon® plates, etc.

Activity 7.3 Animal Food Boxes

Learning objective: Comparison of masses.

Resources: Two plain cardboard boxes, one large and light, one small and heavy; bucket balance.

How to begin: This activity focuses on the attribute of weight, enabling the children to see that the weight of an object is not always determined by its size. Introduce into the vet or pet shop role-play area two boxes of 'animal food'. Ask the children to suggest which box they think will be the heaviest and why, and how they might check. If the children want to hold the boxes, provide them with carrier bags to put each box in to enable them to feel the weight more satisfactorily. Encourage talk using the key vocabulary, and ensuring children have opportunities to use phrases such as 'the big box is lighter than the small box, and the 'small box is heavier than the big box', providing them with the experience of using the opposite term.

Development: Provide a bucket balance for the children to use to explore the masses of the boxes. Use this to stimulate talk about how the balance works and predict what will happen when the boxes are placed inside.

Key vocabulary: Heavier than; lighter than; weighs the same as; balances.

Extension: Encourage the children to measure the mass of each box using uniform or standard units.

 Activity 7.4 Snake Lengths

Learning objective: Understanding of the need for standard units.

Resources: Paper, scissors, metre sticks.

How to begin: Using pet shop role play as a stimulus, for example, suggest that the children make a picture of snakes, or another long creature, for display in the role-play area. Ask the children to suggest how long the snakes might be, for example 6 pencils long. Provide the children with strips of paper and ask them to cut them to the agreed length. Before the children paint them, ask them to compare their lengths with one another and discuss what they notice. This provides them with an opportunity to notice that although they have all worked to an agreed length, their paper snakes will vary, to some extent, in length. Encourage discussion about why this may be and use this as an opportunity to introduce standard units.

Development: Ask the children to measure further strips of paper to an agreed standard length, such as 1 metre, and compare and discuss results. Paint and display snakes.

Key vocabulary: Longer than; shorter than; equal lengths; standard unit; metre; centimetres.

Principles into practice

- Allow young children time to use non-standard units for measuring (books, pencils, bricks, etc.) as they are more likely to be familiar with the required vocabulary and the objects are probably easier to manipulate than standard units. This gives real opportunities for children to become aware of the need for standard units.
- Avoid meaningless measuring: children are more likely to be enthusiastic about measuring something that holds real meaning for them.
- Vary materials used for volume and capacity work to maintain interest and relevance.
- Use balance equipment to measure the mass of objects.
- Be consistent with mathematical vocabulary used for weight and mass, such as 'the bag weighs the same as 20 cubes'.

Examples of independent activities: Pets

Example 7.1   Weighing dog biscuits

Learning context: play tray
Learning objectives:

- Use language such as 'heavier' or 'lighter' to compare objects (ELG)
- Estimate, weigh and compare objects, choosing and using uniform non-standard units and measuring instruments (PNS YI)
- Estimate, compare and measure weights choosing and using standard units and measuring instruments (PNS Y2)

	FS	Y1	Y2
Activity	Children pour and scoop dog biscuits, filling and emptying small hessian sacks. Children explore and discuss whose bag is the heaviest.	As FS, but children use a bucket balance to find the amount of dog biscuits that weighs the same as 20 cubes.	As Y1, but finding bags that weigh the same as 1 kg.
Resources	Assorted dog biscuits; small hessian sacks of different sizes; plastic scoops.	In addition to FS: bucket balance; 20 cubes.	In addition to FS: bucket balance; 1 kg mass.
Prompt and key questions	The pet shop keeper needs to fill the sacks with dog biscuits. Can you help and find out which sack is the heaviest? How can you find out? Do any of the sacks feel as if they weigh the same? Can you put the sacks in order of weight?	The pet shop keeper needs to bag up the dog biscuits. Each bag needs to weigh the same as 20 cubes. What will you do to find the mass of the bags? How do you know each bag weighs the same as 20 cubes?	The pet shop keeper needs to bag up the dog biscuits. Each bag must weigh the same as 1 kg. Can you estimate how many biscuits you will need? What will you do to find the mass accurately? Was your estimate accurate?
Key vocabulary	• heavy • light • heavier than • lighter than • weighs the same as	• heavier than • lighter than • too heavy • too light • weighs the same as • equal • balance • mass	• too heavy • too light • weighs the same as • equal • balance • mass • estimate • accurate • kilogram
Opportunities for assessment	• can use mathematical vocabulary of weight to explain reasoning • can identify accurately which bag is heavier/lighter than a given weight • can compare weights of two bags • can order more than two bags by weight	• can use mathematical vocabulary to explain reasoning • can use bucket balance appropriately • can measure weight with a degree of accuracy	• can use mathematical vocabulary with increasing competence • can give a sensible estimate • can use mathematical apparatus appropriately

Example 7.2   Filling animal water bottles

Learning context: play tray
Learning objectives:

- Use language such as 'greater' or 'smaller' to compare quantities (ELG)
- Estimate, measure and compare objects, choosing and using suitable uniform non-standard units (PNS YI)
- Estimate, compare and measure capacities choosing and using standard units (PNS Y2)

	FS	Y1	Y2
Activity	Children pour water and fill and empty animal water bottles. Discuss and compare the capacities of the bottles.	Children pour water and fill and empty water bottles. They count how many jugs of water it takes to fill each bottle.	Children estimate and explore how many water bottles can be filled using a 1 litre measuring jug.
Resources	Selection of differently sized animal water bottles (600 ml, 100 ml, 350 ml, etc.); small jugs.	As FS.	Four 250 ml water bottles; two 500 ml water bottles; 1 litre measuring jug; clipboard and writing materials.
Prompt and key questions	The pet shop keeper needs to fill the water bottles for the animals. Can you help to fill them and find out which bottle holds the most water, and which bottle holds the least? How can you find out? Which water bottle would be best for a mouse? Why? Which would be best for a big rabbit? Why?	The pet shop keeper needs to fill the water bottles for the animals and find out exactly how much water each bottle holds. Can you find a way to work this out? What are your results? Which bottle held the most and which the least? How much more water did the largest bottle hold compared to the smallest?	The pet shop keeper needs to find out how many water bottles can be filled using 1 litre of water. Estimate how many bottles you think 1 litre will fill and then find out. Can you find a way to record your results? What do your results show?
Key vocabulary	• more • less • most • least • empty • full • nearly full • the same amount • enough • not enough	• more • less • full • almost full • empty • half full • more than • less than • equal amounts • the same as	• full • half full • almost full • quarter full • empty • estimate • litres
Opportunities for assessment	• can use mathematical vocabulary of capacity to describe activity • can compare capacities of two containers • can compare and order capacities of more than two containers	• uses mathematical vocabulary of capacity to describe activity • can measure capacity of bottles and talk about results	• can use mathematical vocabulary of capacity with increasing competence • can give a sensible estimate • can measure and talk about capacity of the bottles

Example 7.3   Homes for snakes and lizards

Learning context: small world drama
Learning objectives:

- Use language such as 'longer than' or 'shorter than' to compare lengths (ELG)
- Estimate, measure and compare objects (PNS Y1)
- Estimate, compare and measure lengths choosing and using standard units and measuring instruments (PNS Y2)

	FS	Y1	Y2
Activity	Children use a selection of materials to make enclosures that are long enough for a chosen plastic creature. Children develop small world play in which key vocabulary is used.	In addition to FS, children make several enclosures of different lengths and sort creatures into them according to their length. Children develop small world play in which key vocabulary is used.	Children select a creature they estimate to be about 10 cm long. They use materials to construct an enclosure long enough for it. Children develop small world play in which key vocabulary is used.
Resources	Green fabric; stones; Pebbles; bark; 'pond' (card covered in silver paper); plastic snakes, newts, lizards of varying lengths.	As FS.	As FS.
Prompt and key questions	The tank in the pet shop has several different creatures who need to have some enclosures made for them. Choose one of the creatures and make a home for it. The home must be long enough. How can you make sure it is long enough? How can you check?	The tank in the pet shop has several creatures of different lengths. They need to have some enclosures made for them. Can you make 3 enclosures of different lengths and sort the creatures into them? How can you make sure they are the right length? How can you check? How many creatures are there in each enclosure?	The pet shop keeper needs to make some enclosures for the creatures in the tank. Can you help by estimating which creatures are about 10 cm long and make an enclosure long enough for them? How many creatures do you think are about 10 cm long? How could you check?
Key vocabulary	• longer than • shorter than • narrower • thicker • wider • about the same • too short • too long • not long enough	• longer than • shorter than • narrower • wider • too short • too long • not long enough • equal lengths	• longer than • shorter than • estimate • equal lengths • centimetres
Opportunities for assessment	• can use mathematical vocabulary of length • can compare two lengths • can compare more than two lengths	• uses mathematical vocabulary of length correctly • can compare more than two lengths • can sort for length	• uses mathematical vocabulary of length with increasing competence • can make sensible estimates

Example 7.4   Making a rabbit cage

Learning context: construction area
Learning objectives:

- Use language such as 'greater' or 'smaller' to compare quantities (ELG)
- Estimate, measure and compare objects, choosing and using suitable uniform non-standard units (PNS Y1)
- Estimate, compare and measure lengths, choosing and using standard units (PNS Y2)

	FS	Y1	Y2
Activity	Children construct a simple cage with Lasy® construction kit which is big enough for a soft toy rabbit to fit into.	As FS, but children estimate how long the cage is and then measure in cubes.	As Y1, but children estimate the length the cage needs to be in centimetres, then measure the constructed cage with a ruler to the nearest centimetre.
Resources	Lasy® construction kit; small soft toy rabbit.	In addition to FS: small uniform cubes.	In addition to FS: centimetre ruler.
Prompt and key questions	The pet shop keeper needs to make a new cage for a rabbit. Can you help by making a cage long enough and wide enough for the rabbit to fit into? What will you need to do to make sure the cage is long enough for the rabbit? How can you test the cage?	The pet shop keeper needs to make a cage for the rabbit. Can you help by making one long enough and wide enough for the rabbit? How long do you think it will have to be? If more cages need to be made, can you find out exactly how long and how wide they should be? What could you use to measure with? Why is this a good choice?	Can you help the pet shop keeper to make a cage big enough for the rabbit? Estimate how long and how wide it will need to be? Measure your cage when you have built it. Was your estimate accurate?
Key vocabulary	• longer than • shorter than • narrower • thicker • wider • too short • too long • not long enough	• longer than • shorter than • narrower • wider • too short • not long enough • is as long as • is as wide as	• estimate • longer than • shorter than • centimetres long • centimetres wide
Opportunities for assessment	• can use mathematical vocabulary of length to explain activity • can compare two lengths • can explain how to test the size of the cage	• can compare two lengths • can make a sensible estimate • can select suitable non-standard units • can use selected units accurately	• can make a sensible estimate • can measure to the nearest centimetre using a ruler

Example 7.5   Snake-making game

Learning context: malleable materials
Learning objectives:

- Use everyday language related to time (PNS FS)
- Use vocabulary related to time (PNS Yl)
- Use units of time and know the relationships between them (PNS Y2)

	FS	Y1	Y2
Activity	Children explore dough and model snakes. They compare with others and count how many they have made during one minute, as measured by the sand timer.	As FS.	As FS.
Resources	Modelling dough; one-minute sand timer.	As FS.	In addition to FS: a written label asking 'How many snakes can you make in 1 minute?'
Prompt and key questions	How many snakes do you think you can make in 1 minute? Find out how many you can make before the sand runs out. Who has made the most? Do you make the same number each time?	How many snakes do you think you might make in 1 minute? Did you make the same number of snakes each time? How many do you think you might make in 2 minutes?	As Y1.
Key vocabulary	• before • while • after • next • minute	• before • after • during • minute	• before • after • during • minute
Opportunities for assessment	• can use vocabulary of time appropriately • demonstrates an understanding of when the activity begins and ends	• can use vocabulary of time appropriately • can use sand timer appropriately • shows an understanding of two minutes being twice as long	• can use vocabulary of time appropriately • can use sand timer appropriately • shows an understanding of two minutes being twice as long

Example 7.6   Appointments at the vets

Learning context: role play
Learning objectives:

- Use everyday language related to time; order and sequence familiar events (PNS FS)
- Use vocabulary related to time; order days of the week (PNS YI)
- Use units of time and know the relationships between them (PNS Y2)

	FS	Y1	Y2
Activity	Children engage in vet surgery role play, using resources to write appointment cards, write opening and closing times, call patients and keep appointment book.	As FS.	As FS.
Resources	Soft toy animals; bandages; stethoscope; telephone; till; money; calendar; analogue clock; appointment cards; appointment book; opening and closing time sign; dressing up clothes; writing materials.	As FS.	As FS.
Prompt and key questions	The pet owners need to know what day and time to bring their pet again. The vet needs to know which animal to see first. Who is next? Who went before? How long will the bandage need to stay on for? When is your next appointment?	As FS.	The pet owners need to know when to bring their pets to the surgery. Can you write some appointment cards? What day and at what time will the animal have to come? Is that later or earlier than the last appointment?
Key vocabulary	• later • tomorrow • yesterday • days of the week • months • before • next • afterwards • weekend • morning • afternoon • evening	• days of the week • month names • weekend • morning • afternoon • evening • yesterday • tomorrow • minutes • hour • o'clock times	• days of the week • month names • weekend • fortnight • yesterday • tomorrow • minutes • hour • half an hour • quarter of an hour • o'clock times
Opportunities for assessment	• can sequence events in role play • uses vocabulary of time	• can sequence events in role play • uses vocabulary of time with increasing competence	• uses vocabulary of time with increasing competence • can read and write o'clock and half past times

Suggested further reading 📖

Blinko, J. and Slater, A. (1996) *Teaching Measures: Activities, Organization and Management*. London: Hodder-Stoughton.

Leather, R. (2000) *Developing Space, Shape and Measures with 5–7-Year-Olds*. Leamington Spa: Scholastic.

Montague-Smith, A. (2002) *Mathematics Education in the Nursery*, 2nd edition. London: David Fulton Publishers.

Pepperell, S., Hopkins, C., Gifford, S. and Tallant, T. (2009) *Mathematics in the Primary School: A Sense of Progression*. London: Routledge.

Rhydderch-Evans, Z. (1993) *Mathematics in the School Grounds*. Devon: Southgate Publishers.

8

Planning, organizing and assessing independent play

> **This chapter covers:**
> - planning for playful mathematics teaching and independent play
> - adult involvement in play
> - assessing, recording and reporting
> - photocopiable material to help with planning and assessment.

Planning

While guidance for mathematics planning is given in detail in a variety of documents and websites (see Resources), this chapter focuses on planning mathematics teaching with meaningful connection-making in mind, and for independent play. As with all effective planning, practitioners need to assess where children are in terms of their own mathematical development, determined by observation and formative assessment, and where they need to go next. The planning of 'where next' can be set in playful and meaningful context by considering what the children's current interests are, or establishing a unifying learning theme.

Planning for a playful and meaningful context for mathematics teaching

Observing what motivates children, what they become involved in and what captures their imagination, informs practitioners of a suitable creative context in which to set the mathematics teaching. Figure 8.1 illustrates some questions that practitioners might explore to help realize the mathematical potential of a variety of activities and how they can make links with other areas of learning. If these links with other learning areas are established, children are more able to make connections and make sense of their learning.

Planning for independent play

Once a creative context or theme has been decided upon, then planning for continuous provision and independent play can begin.

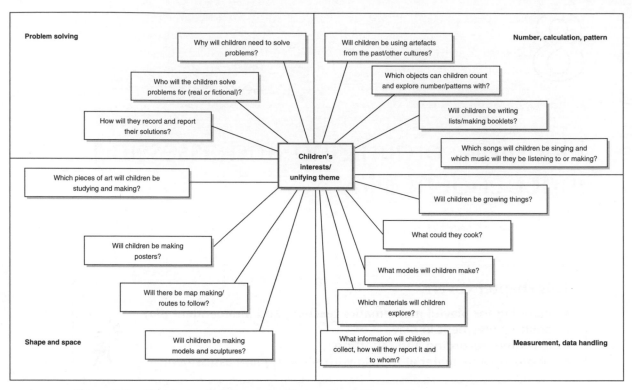

Figure 8.1   Planning a creative context for mathematics teaching

Planning checklist for independent play

- What learning objectives need to be addressed in order to extend learning?
- What are the children's current interests, or learning theme?
- What mathematical opportunities does this offer (counting, pattern making, weighing, using money etc.)?
- Which learning context best facilitates these (small world, play tray etc.)?
- What resources are needed?
- How might the children use these resources?
- What prompt and key questions will stimulate play and promote learning?
- Does the activity encourage cooperation and talk and promote sustained shared thinking?
- Will there be any visible outcome?
- When will the children be able to talk about what they have done, or show any recorded graphics, and evaluate what they have done?

Planning for independent play should be recorded in ways that are helpful to the practitioner and reflect their intended learning outcomes. Figure 8.2 and Figure 8.3 are examples of planning for play and independent activity for Foundation Stage and Key Stage 1 (see Photocopiable Sheets 1 and 2). The plans are:

- intended for a three-week period

- linked to areas of learning and development in the Foundation Stage and show links to areas of learning in Key Stage 1

- based on the theme of 'the sea'.

The practitioner cannot, of course, plan for child-initiated activity, as this will happen spontaneously, but the aim is to provide resources that motivate this. These activities and learning intentions can then be 'advertised' to the children, as seen in Figure 8.4. As the plans are thematic in nature, and show links between several learning areas, the practitioner can identify and highlight specific mathematical activity for the inclusion in weekly planning or individual session plans (see Tables 8.2–8.4).

Planning for playful mathematics sessions

As previously discussed, child-initiated play and independent mathematical activity alone do not provide the systematic repeated experience and practice needed to ensure progression. Focused teaching groups must also be playful and meaningful; the adults should be actively teaching and subject-secure so that they can plan for progression (DCSF, 2008; Gifford, 2008; Siraj-Blatchford et al., 2002). As we have seen in Chapter 1, mathematics teaching and learning can be provided for by the mix of focused teaching and independent play. Tables 8.1–8.4 are exemplars of differentiated mathematics session plans for Reception to Year 2. Table 8.1 is an exemplar of a short session that can be used in conjunction with any of the exemplars. Tables 8.2–8.4 are exemplars of session plans that show focused teaching alongside independent play and which:

- use PNS learning objectives and ELGs

- provide ideas for resources in the playful context of 'the sea'

- act as a guide to illustrate how a session might be adapted and extended from Reception to Year 2

- follow the session structure illustrated in Figure 1.2.

- **Learning opportunities and curriculum links**

Ice-cream kiosk

Developing related narrative, writing price lists/shop signs (CLL/lit); counting/sorting spoons, ice-cream tubs and cones, etc.; writing prices on items to sell; reading numerals on price lists/telephone and telephone book; using coins to make values and give change (PSRN/maths); using maps to give directions (KUW/geography)

- **Resources**

Writing materials; till; coins; telephone and telephone directory; calendar; clock; bags and purses; assorted ice-cream tubs/cartons; paper cones; assorted spoons and ice-cream scoop; maps and postcards; dressing-up clothes

Role play

- **Learning opportunities and curriculum links**

Journey to the seaside

Developing narrative (CLL/lit); designing and making train layout, using positional/geographical language (PSRN, KUW/maths, geography); counting/sorting/making patterns with vehicles and farm animals (PSRN/maths)

The Bear's Adventure

Developing own narrative and retelling story (CLL/lit); counting/sorting/making patterns with shells/farm animals (PSRN/lit); using positional and geographical language (PSRN, KUW, CD/lit, geography)

- **Resources**

Train track; farm animals; fencing; vehicles; play people; shells; pebbles; driftwood; teddy; sea animals; boats; buildings

Small world drama

- **Learning opportunities and curriculum links**

Marble run of chosen number; counting/ ordering/matching to numeral 0–10 staircase using acorns, shells, doubloons; making chosen number using Numicon® (PSRN/maths); marble run chosen letter; letter-matching games (CLL/lit)

- **Resources**

Marble runs; acorns; shells; number lines 0–10; Numicon®

Table-top activity

- **Learning opportunities and curriculum links**

Reading big sentence maker; reading in book corner a selection of self-chosen books; reading book of the week; reading labels and signs in the environment; listening to a selection of story tapes and rhymes (CLL/lit)

- **Resources**

Book of the week; selection of story tapes

Reading and listening activity

Figure 8.2 Independent play

Creative and aesthetic

- **Learning opportunities and curriculum links**
  Modelling and painting chosen letter (CLL, PD, CD/lit); modelling and painting chosen numeral (PSRN, PD, CD/maths); modelling/counting/sorting/sharing and grouping dough shells and treasure (PD,PSRN/maths); painting characters in book of the week (CD, CLL/maths, art); painting historical seaside artefacts (CD, KUW/art, history)

- **Resources**
  Modelling dough; paint; book of the week; historical resources

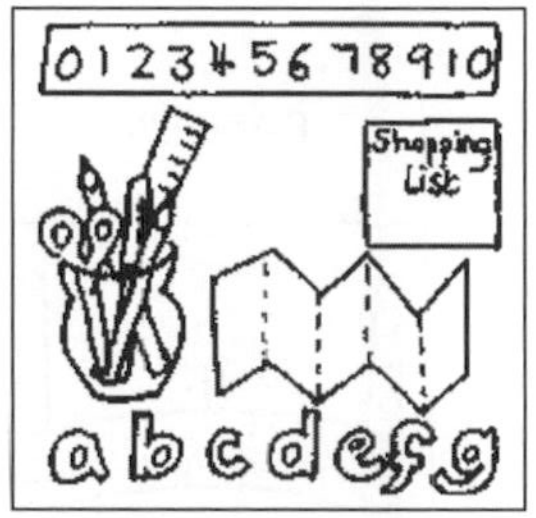

Graphics area

- **Learning opportunities and curriculum links**
  Making booklets about chosen letter/word/book; writing lists and postcards (CLL/lit); making booklets about chosen number/shapes/things longer and shorter than; filling in empty number lines; ordering numerals (PSRN/maths); drawing and making maps for pirates (CLL, KUW/lit, geography)

- **Resources**
  Paper; staples; scissors; glue sticks; writing materials; numbered and empty number lines; sheets of numerals 0–20; rulers

ICT

- **Learning opportunities and curriculum links**
  Using a selection of simple computer programs to create signs/price lists for ice-cream kiosk (KUW, PSRN, CD/ICT)

- **Resources**
  2Simple paint program

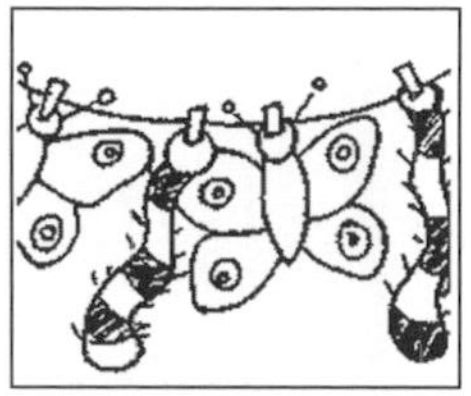

Washing line

- **Learning opportunities and curriculum links**
  Ordering numeral cards; finding missing numeral in a sequence; making patterns with sea-related pictures (PSRN/maths); ordering historical postcards (KUW/history)

- **Resources**
  Numeral cards 0–10/0–20; sea postcards; pictures of seaside artefacts; old postcards of holidays in the past

Figure 8.2 Independent play

(Continued)

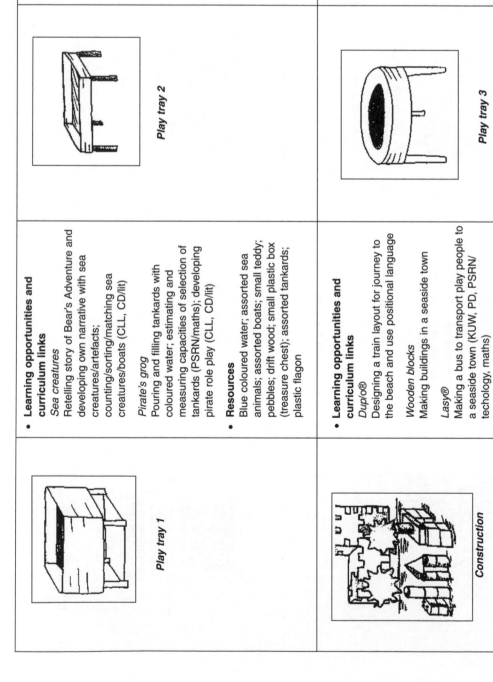

- **Learning opportunities and curriculum links**
  Sea creatures
  Retelling story of Bear's Adventure and developing own narrative with sea creatures/artefacts; counting/sorting/matching sea creatures/boats (CLL, CD/lit)

  Pirate's grog
  Pouring and filling tankards with coloured water; estimating and measuring capacities of selection of tankards (PSRN/maths); developing pirate role play (CLL, CD/lit)

- **Resources**
  Blue coloured water; assorted sea animals; assorted boats; small teddy; pebbles; drift wood; small plastic box (treasure chest); assorted tankards; plastic flagon

Play tray 1

- **Learning opportunities and curriculum links**
  Mirrors
  Using mirrors and half pictures of boats to explore reflection and symmetry (PSRN, KUW/maths, science)

  Coloured telescopes
  Using cardboard telescopes and coloured transparent paper to view through and discuss how colours change (KUW/science)

- **Resources**
  Pairs of toy sea creatures; half pictures of boats on card; mirrors; cardboard cylinders; sticky tape; transparent coloured gel

Play tray 2

- **Learning opportunities and curriculum links**
  Duplo®
  Designing a train layout for journey to the beach and use positional language

  Wooden blocks
  Making buildings in a seaside town

  Lasy®
  Making a bus to transport play people to a seaside town (KUW, PD, PSRN/techology, maths)

- **Resources**
  Duplo®f; wooden bricks; Lasy®

Construction

- **Learning opportunities and curriculum links**
  Sea rubbish
  Exploring a selection of beach 'rubbish' with magnets, sorting items that are/are not magnetic (KUW, PSRN, CLL/science)

  Telescopes and binoculars
  Making telescopes and binoculars for pirates using cutting and joining skills (PD, KUW, PSRN/technology)

- **Resources**
  Selection of magnetic/non-magnetic items and packaging; cardboard cylinders; sticky tape; scissors; pens

Play tray 3

Figure 8.2 Independent play

Role play

- **Learning opportunities and curriculum**

  Bus journey

  Developing narrative about bus journey to the seaside; writing tickets (CD, CLL/lit); buying tickets, finding amounts and giving change (PSRN/maths); using positional and geographical language to describe journey (KUW/geography)

  Pirates' voyage

  Developing narrative about voyage, writing about journey/weather in log book (CLL, CD/lit); counting/sorting/capacity work with treasure; counting/sharing/grouping doubloons (PSRN/maths); drawing maps and using positional and geographical language (KUW, PSRN/maths, geography)

- **Resources**

  Dressing-up clothes; money, writing materials; wooden blocks; pirate dressing-up clothes; tankards; 'treasure and doubloons'; maps; treasure chest; telescopes; log book

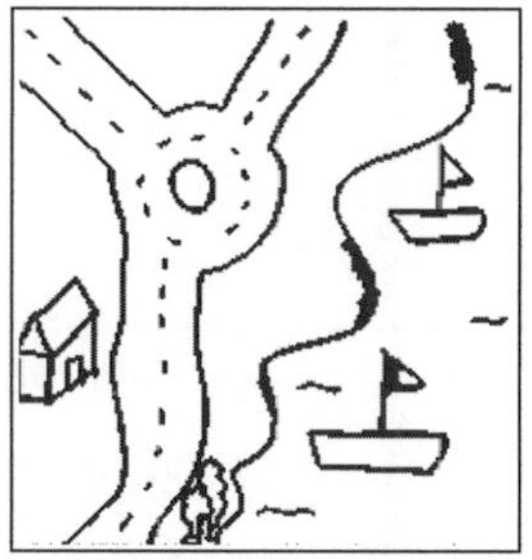

Small world drama

- **Learning opportunities and curriculum links**

  Seaside town where children explore routes for play people to travel to the beach using positional and geographical language and developing narrative (KUW, CLL, PSRN/geography)

- **Resources**

  Train track; selection of vehicles; small wooden buildings; play-people; boats; lighthouse; blue and brown pieces of fabric; pebbles; shells; driftwood

Table-top activity

- **Learning opportunities and curriculum links**

  Counting doubloons in groups of 10; putting each group of 10 in a 'chest' (PSRN/maths)

- **Resources**

  'Doubloons'; cardboard box 'chests'

Reading and listening activity

- **Learning opportunities and curriculum links**

  Reading a selection of fiction and non-fiction sea books (CLL/lit)

- **Resources**

  Selected books from book area

Figure 8.3   Independent play in the outside play area

(Continued)

(Continued)

Creative and aesthetic area

- **Learning opportunities and curriculum links**
  Painting chosen letter/word; painting characters from book of the week (CLL/lit); painting chosen number (PSRN/maths); painting in response to Andy Goldsworthy's work (CD/art)
- **Resources**
  Paint; paper; card

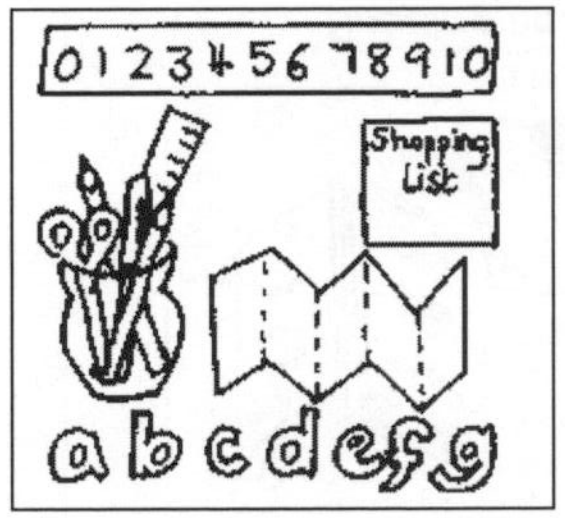

Graphics area

- **Learning opportunities and curriculum links**
  Writing road signs for bus journey role play, bus tickets and signs; writing letters to pirates and in log books (CLL/lit); drawing maps (KUW/geography); writing number of the week; writing price lists for bus tickets (PSRN/maths)
- **Resources**
  Pens; card; scissors; sheets of photocopied numerals 0–20; numbered in sand and empty number lines

Garden

- **Learning opportunities and curriculum links**
  Selecting watering can to fill and water hyacinths (KUW, PSRN/science, maths)
- **Resources**
  Graduated watering cans

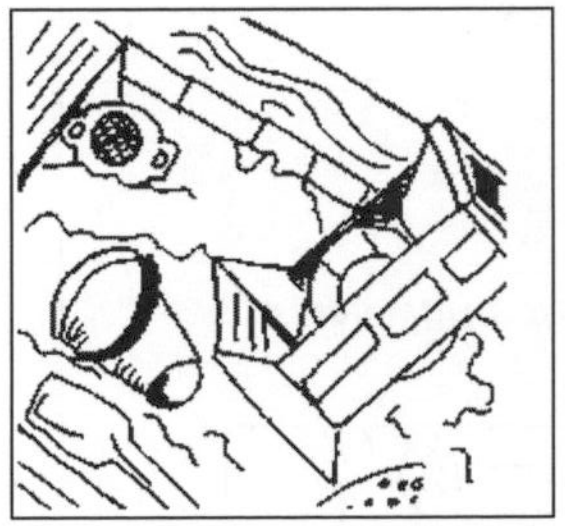

Sandpit

- **Learning opportunities and curriculum links**
  Making letter/word of the week and driving car/truck around shape made (CLL/lit); making chosen number and driving car/truck around shape (PSRN/maths); pouring/filling; exploring capacity; estimating and measuring (PSRN/maths)
- **Resources**
  Selection of buckets and containers; rakes; small cars and trucks

Figure 8.3 Independent play in the outside play area

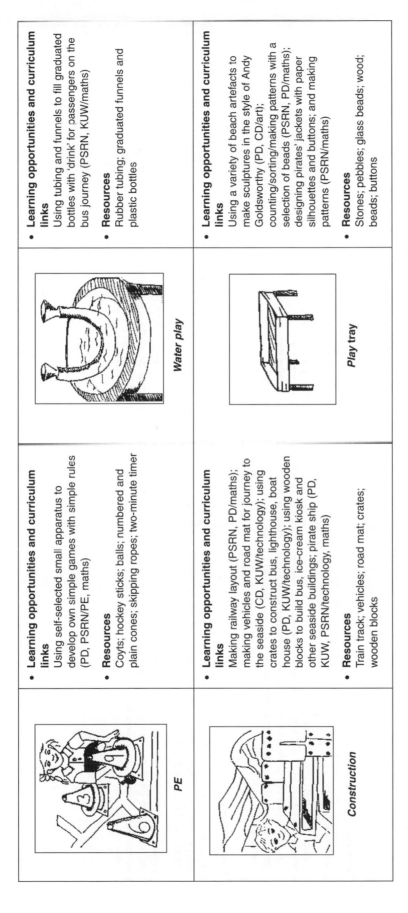

The content of the figure, read as four quadrants:

PE

- **Learning opportunities and curriculum links**
  Using self-selected small apparatus to develop own simple games with simple rules (PD, PSRN/PE, maths)

- **Resources**
  Coyts; hockey sticks; balls; numbered and plain cones; skipping ropes; two-minute timer

Water play

- **Learning opportunities and curriculum links**
  Using tubing and funnels to fill graduated bottles with 'drink' for passengers on the bus journey (PSRN, KUW/maths)

- **Resources**
  Rubber tubing; graduated funnels and plastic bottles

Construction

- **Learning opportunities and curriculum links**
  Making railway layout (PSRN, PD/maths); making vehicles and road mat for journey to the seaside (CD, KUW/technology); using crates to construct bus, lighthouse, boat house (PD, KUW/technology); using wooden blocks to build bus, ice-cream kiosk and other seaside buildings; pirate ship (PD, KUW, PSRN/technology, maths)

- **Resources**
  Train track; vehicles; road mat; crates; wooden blocks

Play tray

- **Learning opportunities and curriculum links**
  Using a variety of beach artefacts to make sculptures in the style of Andy Goldsworthy (PD, CD/art); counting/sorting/making patterns with a selection of beads (PSRN, PD/maths); designing pirates' jackets with paper silhouettes and buttons; and making patterns (PSRN/maths)

- **Resources**
  Stones; pebbles; glass beads; wood; beads; buttons

Figure 8.3 Independent play in the outside play area

Table 8.1 Mental/oral calculation

Learning objectives:	Key vocabulary:	Resources:
• Count aloud in 1s and 10s (PNS FS) • Count on or back in 1s and 10s and use this knowledge to derive multiples of 10 (Y1) • Count in 10s and explain what each digit represents in a two-digit number and derive and recall all addition and subtraction facts for all pairs of multiples of 10 with totals up to 100 (Y2)	• Counting on/counting back • More/greater than • Less/smaller than • 10s and 1s • partition	• Counting stick • Small world fish • Digit flip books 0–100/whiteboards and pens

Direct teaching

Indicate the 0 and 100 end of the counting stick and explain that the fish is going to swim along its length, 'resting' at the marks which represent a 10s number. Children count in 10s from 0 to 100 and back. Rest the fish in the middle of the stick. Ask the children to indicate on flip books or whiteboards which number the fish is resting on and to discuss and explain how they know it must be 50. Rest the fish at other intervals along the stick and ask the children to indicate which number it represents and to explain their thinking.

Extension: Ask the children to indicate the number which is 10 more or less than the number where the fish rests. Ask them to indicate the number that is its partner to make 100, then count on to check. Rest the fish in between two marks and ask the children to calculate what number its position represents. Ask them to discuss their reasoning and to partition their answer into 10s and 1s.

Table 8.2   Session focus: addition and subtraction

Learning objectives:

- Begin to relate addition to combining two groups of objects and subtraction as 'take away' (ELG)
- Relate addition to counting on and recognize that addition can be done in any order (Y1)
- Understand that subtraction is the inverse of addition and vice versa (Y2)

Key vocabulary: counting on/counting back; more/greater than; less/smaller than; adding; subtracting; take away; equals; the same as
Resources: 10 small world fishes; small nets; large blue cloth (the 'sea'); large floor number line 0 to 10; individual number lines 0 to 10; Numicon®; whiteboards and pens

Introduction and direct teaching	Focused teaching/Guided group work	Independent work
Make explicit the learning objectives and key vocabulary in the context of a fisherman making 2 catches of fish. Explain that the task is to find out how many fish the fisherman catches, and to keep a 'record'. Using the nets, make 2 catches, ensuring that the numbers in each are different. How many fish are there altogether? Repeat with different numbers making reference to the number line. Model correct algorithms as a 'record'.	Ask each child in turn to make 2 catches and combine the 2 groups to determine how many altogether. Relate this to a large floor as before. Repeat using different numbers, reinforcing that 2 groups can be combined in any order. Introduce the idea of fish escaping to illustrate subtraction as 'take away' and relate to floor number line by jumping back.	Play tray: Can you make a record of the fish you catch with the nets? Modelling materials: Make 2 groups of sea creatures. Can you record how many you have altogether? Graphics area: Can you make a poster advertising the best 2 catches of the day. How many fish are there?
Extension: Relate this to the floor number line by asking a child to relate the addition of 2 groups to jumps along the floor number line. Explore the outcome if the catches are added in a different order, again relating to the number line.	Extension: Explain that 4 fish and 3 fish are caught making a total of 7. Then 3 fish escape. Use jumps forwards and back along the number line and the groups of fish and overlay the corresponding Numicon® plates to demonstrate images and connections between the inverse relationship.	Table top: Take 2 pieces of Numicon® from the bag (0–10) and use them to help record a fish addition and subtraction story.
Introduce independent play activities and direct groups.		

Review time and plenary: Ask a group of children to discuss and review their independent work.
Probing question: Can you show and talk about the connection between addition and subtraction using 2 groups of fish?

Table 8.3 Session focus: estimating, counting and place value

Learning objectives:

- Count reliably up to 10 everyday objects (ELG). Estimate how many objects they can see and check by counting (PNS FS)
- Use knowledge of place value to position numbers, 0–20, on a number line (Y1)
- Count up to 100 objects by grouping in 10s and explain what each digit in a two-digit number represents (Y2)

Key vocabulary: estimate; guess; more than/less than; 10s and 1s; partition; more than/greater than; in between
Resources: *The Lighthouse Keeper's Lunch* (see Resources); IWB; 100 'breadsticks' (short lengths of art straws, or similar); 10 bundles of 10 'breadsticks'; 10 paper plates; dice; number lines, both numbered and empty; whiteboards and pens

Introduction and direct teaching	Focused teaching/Guided group work	Independent work
Remind the children about the story of the Grinlings and how Mrs Grinling prepares lunch for Mr Grinling. Make explicit the learning objectives and key vocabulary in the context of Mrs Grinling putting breadsticks in bundles of 10. Use the IWB with images of breadsticks and ask the children to estimate how many breadsticks they can see. What would be a quick way to count them? Ask a child to count and collect 10 breadsticks together. Count the resultant 'bundles' in 10s.	Give each child a handful of 'breadsticks'. Ask them to estimate how many they have and to compare estimates with others. Ask them to check their estimate by counting. Was it more or less than their estimate? Ask them to find the number on the number line. Was anyone's estimate accurate? Whose was the closest?	Play tray: How many fishes do you think there are? Can you put fishes in bags of 10? Can you count in 10s how many there are?

Modelling materials: Can you make 10 pieces of food for Mr Grinling? |
| Introduce independent activities and direct groups. | Extension: Mrs Grinling introduces a game to make it fun to pack the breadsticks. Each child rolls a dice, collects the corresponding number of breadsticks and records the number. When 10 breadsticks are gathered, they are exchanged for a bundle of 10. Reinforce that 21, for example, is 2 bundles of 10 and a 1.Discuss how this is written and what each digit represents. At the end of the game, children count their total number in 10s, write the number and position it on the empty number line representing 0 to 100. Ask them to discuss their reasoning and to partition their number into 10s and 1s. | Washing line: Can you hang these numbers (random numbers from 0 to 100) on the 'pulley' in the right order?

Role play: Mrs Grinling would like to set the table with 10 pieces of food on each plate.

Table top: Take a handful of shells, estimate how many you have and then count accurately. Write the number and place it where you think it is on an empty number line. |

Review time and plenary: Ask a group of children to discuss and review their independent work. Count 23 breadsticks, for example, in bundles of 10s and 1s.
Probing question: Can you partition into 10s and 1s and say which digit is worth more, the 3 or the 2?

Table 8.4 Session focus: space, position and turns

Learning objectives:

- Use everyday words to describe position (ELG)
- Recognise and make whole, half and quarter turns (Y1)
- Recognise and make whole, half and quarter turns both clockwise and anti-clockwise (Y2)

Key vocabulary: forwards; backwards; sideways; left; right; whole; half; quarter turns; clockwise; anti-clockwise
Resources: PIXIE (or similar programmable toy); large sheet of thick blue paper (the 'sea') with grid drawn on (each square the same length as PIXIE); small world boats/lighthouses/sea creatures, etc; large paper circle, semi-circle and quarter circle; vocabulary cards for key vocabulary (above); captain's hat (or similar)

Introduction and direct teaching	Focused teaching/Guided group work	Independent work
Make explicit the learning objectives in the context of a boat lost at sea that needs directions. Place small world objects around the floor and ask a child to be the captain. Modelling key vocabulary, give the child directions to cross the floor, avoiding the obstacles.	Ask children around 'the sea' grid to position the small world objects. Encourage them to describe where they are placing the objects in relation to other objects and children. Put a play person on top of PIXIE; this is the captain on the lost boat.	Small world drama: make up a story about the lost boat. What does it find on its journey? Draw and describe to a friend a picture map of the scene for the log book.
	Using the grid, ask the children to estimate how far they need to send 'the boat' from one object to the next. Encourage them to use key vocabulary to describe their route, and then program PIXIE to follow it.	Role play: give directions to the captain (development of 'instant' role play from direct teaching scenario).
Extension: introduce whole, half and quarter turns, clockwise and anti-clockwise vocabulary. Lay chosen paper shape on the floor to act as a 'turn silhouette' for the child to move around to encourage understanding of whole, quarter, half.		Graphics area: draw a map/write directions to tell the boat how to get out of the fog. Tell a friend.
		Table-top: use the 2D shapes to make a picture of the missing boat and the scene.
Introduce independent work and direct groups.	Extension: using the vocabulary cards to ensure key vocabulary is used, children work in pairs. One child gives directions, while the other programs PIXIE accordingly.	

Review time and plenary: Ask a group of children to discuss and review their independent work. Encourage children to use key vocabulary when describing resultant maps or written directions.

Organizing play

As seen in Chapter 2, the learning environment plays an important role in promoting good quality teaching and learning, both in its content and organization. While Chapter 1 considered a possible structure for teaching mathematics through play for a mixed-age class, its management will be considered here. In terms of the day-to-day running of a busy classroom, the children need to know which of the learning contexts in the continuous provision are available to them, what they might 'do' in these contexts (the practitioners' intended learning outcomes), and the expectations of how they are to be used, including transition from one context to the next. These learning contexts and associated learning intentions, or prompts, therefore need to be made known to the children, while the number of children visiting each context should be monitored to avoid crushes in one particular area. This can be achieved in a variety of ways:

- A 'play board' or 'play menu' can be used (see Figure 8.4). Here, drawings or photographs of the learning contexts are posted alongside the practitioner's written prompt with questions to stimulate play. Once they have been explained to the children, they act as a visual reminder. Some practitioners encourage the children to indicate which contexts they have visited, by writing their name beside each picture or attaching a named peg. This also acts as a means of recording which learning contexts the child has visited during the day or week.

- Sashes, badges or posters can be used to inform children about how many of them can use a particular context at any one time. If it is practical to have a maximum of four children at a particular play tray, for example, then four sashes or clip-on badges might be made available for the children to put on when they visit this area. Once the sashes are all being used, the context is 'full'. Similarly, posters at each context can remind the children of suitable participant numbers, the most successful of which show the numeral, the written word and an array of the number.

Adult involvement

As seen in Chapter 2, adult intervention through talk and questioning is most effective when done appropriately and sensitively. Adults, whether professionals or parent helpers, can be involved in play in a variety of ways:

- Visiting adults and parent helpers can be effective in helping to extend and support mathematical development once they understand the nature of the play the child is engaged in, and the learning intentions the practitioner has planned for each learning context. Attaching the written prompt and key questions beside each learning context not only helps to reinforce this for the children, but also acts as a means of communicating to adults the nature of the intended activity. When starting statutory schooling, children may lack the requisite skills to select and use learning contexts appropriately, and

• Can you use the Lasy to make a bus big enough to carry 5 people to the seaside?
• Can you make a bus big enough to carry double the number of passengers?

The pirates need to find out how many tankards a full flagon of grog will fill.
• Can you help and find out how many?
• Can you find a way of recording your results?

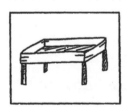

• How do the sea pictures change when you hold a mirror against them?
• Can you make your own symmetrical sea picture? Fold it in half and use a mirror!

• Can you help sort the beach rubbish for recycling?
• How many things are magnetic?
• Can you find a way to record which things are magnetic and which are not?

Figure 8.4   Independent play menu

(Continued)

(Continued)

• Can you make some price tags for things in the kiosk?

• You have 20p to spend in the kiosk What will you buy?

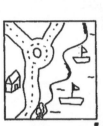

On the train to the seaside the passengers notice the farm animals are in a pattern

• Can you put the animals in a pattern?

• What sort of pattern is it?

• Can you paint **5** pirates?

• The pirate finds **5** pieces of treasure Can you use the dough to make them? Can you make double the number?

• Can you use the shells to make a number staircase? What do you notice?

• Can you use the things on the table to find different ways of making **5**?

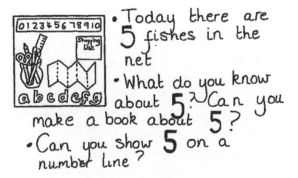

• Today there are **5** fishes in the net

• What do you know about **5**? Can you make a book about **5**?

• Can you show **5** on a number line?

Figure 8.4   Independent play menu

so by having written intentions immediately available for adults to see, they can help to support the youngest children as they learn the routines of the environment.

- Practitioners should plan opportunities where they are available to talk to children about their involvement in play and ask open questions, thus addressing a balance of practitioner and child agendas. This in turn will aid assessment.

- Adults can take digital photographs, or mini films, of play. Once again, this shows the children that adults are both interested in and value what they are doing. These can act as records of the activity for displays and portfolios.

Assessing, recording and reporting

Opportunities for assessing independent play will arise when:

- target observations are made of a specific child, group of children or a learning context during play

- there is sustained shared thinking

- children report back at review time or as part of a plenary.

During these situations, practitioners can note:

- whether children are interacting and talking with others

- mathematical vocabulary children are using

- how children are using resources

- whether children are involved in practitioner-initiated or self-initiated play (Have they extended the practitioner-initiated play to suit their own purpose, or developed their own entirely?)

- which learning outcomes have been reached.

Recorded observations of play can be matched to assessment criteria to show the practitioner 'where the child is' and 'where the child needs to go next', thus informing planning. They can take the form of:

- brief observations and annotated photos

- notes made on a pro forma (see Photocopiable 3), which constitutes part of a child's ongoing assessments, aspects of which can be used to inform the recording in the Early Years Foundation Stage Profile.

Assessments will also be made during review time where four to six children in a large class can report back on their independent play. This allows the practitioner to assess the child's involvement in the activity, along with the success of the planned continuous provision. Figure 8.5 is an example of recorded assessments made during this time. A blank version of this sheet has been provided for your own use (see Photocopiable 4). Practitioners will need to report children's progress to parents and this is considered in Chapter 9.

Date	Name	Nature of work reviewed	Learning objective addressed
3/11	Ben	Small world drama. Described how each pirate's chest had 2 pieces of treasure and recorded accurately as: 2 + 2 + 2 + 2 + 2 = 10.	Understands that more than 2 groups can be added together.
3/11	Emily	Graphics area. Drew a number line from 0 to 11 and marked all odd numbers.	Shows understanding of difference between odd and even numbers.
3/11	Lois	Graphics area. Drew own number line from 0 to 15.	Writes and orders numbers beyond 10.
3/11	Edward	Table-top. Uses Numicon and shells to explore ways of making 8. Recorded algorithms, mostly correct.	Writes addition facts of 8.
4/11	Isaac	Play tray. Explains that a flagon of grog will fill 3 tankards. Uses vocabulary such as: full, holds, fills, the same as.	Uses vocabulary of capacity.

Figure 8.5   Record and assessment sheet for review time

Children's self-assessment

Involving children in their self-assessment gives the practitioner a greater understanding of the child, and allows the child to see themselves as an individual who can make and discuss their own discoveries and ideas. Questions such as 'What do you like best?', 'What are you good at?' and 'What do you find hard?' often lead to a reflective discussion. Starting points for reflective discussion and self-assessment include:

- looking through the child's portfolio or learning journey

- looking together at annotated photos of mathematical activity

- a review time when the child reports back on independent play.

Creative ideas for good practice

- Select a motivating theme, based on children's interests in which to set mathematics (both in focused teaching sessions and in independent play), which allows good cross-curricular links to be made.
- Plan independent play and activity carefully, identifying learning objectives or outcomes, an appropriate learning context to facilitate these, suitable resources and imaginative ways for children to record outcomes (if appropriate).
- Ensure children know which learning contexts are available to them, how they are to be used and the planned learning intentions.
- Involve adults in supporting children in their play by planning time for them to observe children at play and to make sensitive interactions.
- Allow children time to report back about their play, to share what they have discovered or what they were reminded about.
- Make assessments of children's mathematical development through observations of their play, interactions with them, and during their reporting back.

Suggested further reading

Carr, M. (2001) *Assessment in Early Childhood Settings: Learning Stories.* London: Paul Chapman Publishing.

DfES (2007) *Creating the Picture.* London: DfES.

Drummond, M-J. (2003) *Assessing Children's Learning*, 2nd edition. London: David Fulton Publishing.

Fisher, J. (2002) *Starting From the Child.* Buckingham: Open University Press.

Hutchin, V. (2003) *Observing and Assessing for the Foundation Stage Profile.* London: Hodder Murray.

Montague-Smith, A. (2002) *Mathematics Education in the Nursery*, 2nd edition. London: David Fulton Publishers.

Wood, E. and Atfield, J. (2005) *Play, Learning and the Early Childhood Curriculum*, 2nd edition. London: Paul Chapman Publishing.

9

Parents as partners: involving parents in mathematics and play

---

This chapter covers:

- a brief discussion of the role of parental involvement as described in recent legislation
- the benefits of involving parents in their child's mathematical education
- family learning programmes
- strategies for involving parents in their child's early years mathematics education.

Why work with parents?

If children are to perceive themselves as capable mathematicians, then they need to feel confident and positive about themselves as learners and doers of mathematics. Involving parents in their child's mathematics education plays a significant part in how a child feels about and engages with the subject. Partnership with parents has a high profile in the EYFS and *The Children's Plan: Building Brighter Futures* (DCSF, 2007) states:

> Partnership with parents is a unifying theme of this Children's Plan. Our vision of 21st century children's services is that they should engage parents in all aspects of their children's development, and children's services should be shaped by parents' views and command parents' confidence. (DCSF, 2007: 57)

Indeed, there is evidence (Desforges, 2003) to suggest that differences in parental involvement have a greater impact on a child's achievement than differences associated with variations in the quality of schooling at primary age. What parents can do with their children at home has far greater significance than any other factor open to educational influence. Problems associated with parental involvement, however, often arise because many parents are influenced by their own experience of mathematics education and find it difficult to re-engage with the process. While parents who are confident with maths and eager to help their child will have a positive impact on the child as learner, it follows that parents who have not enjoyed a good relationship with the subject, and who feel 'no good' at maths, may have a negative impact on their child's learning. In this case, it seems likely that the child will grow to believe maths is 'hard and boring'; there is a clear link between parents with low-level mathematical skills and their children's underachievement in mathematics (DCSF, 2008). Without positive intervention, therefore, it is all too easy to see how a cycle of underachievement in mathematics might be perpetuated. The key, then, to empowering children to view themselves as mathematicians is for practitioners and teachers to provide opportunities for parents to reassess their relationship with mathematics. If parents can begin to realize that mathematics can be creative, exciting and fun, they may then believe attainment in the subject is desirable and achievable.

It is, in fact, their child's level of attainment in mathematics that strongly influences the level of parental involvement. If a parent is given the opportunity to see their child 'being a mathematician' (see below), they are then more likely to want to become involved themselves (Desforges, 2003). There have been several projects whose aim has been to raise children's attainment in mathematics through parental involvement, notably the Ocean Maths Project (cited in DCSF, 2008). The success of this project, and others, has been to involve parents in workshops that aim to help adults enjoy maths activities and to change their attitudes to maths both at home, school and in the community. Young children often act as 'mathematical connection-makers', making links between the mathematical experiences they have had in the home and those they have at school. Such projects provide parents with a window into this 'connection-making' process, thus enabling them to support their child's mathematical development with greater understanding and confidence.

Promoting parents' involvement with their child's maths can:

- encourage them to have a more positive approach to the subject

- help bring parents up to date with current strategies and approaches

- provide parents with the shared language of mathematics

- enable parents to discover the cumulative nature of mathematics and its progression

- allow parents to see their child as a capable mathematician

- encourage a shared interest in the subject with their child.

Family learning programmes

At its most literal, these programmes bring family members together to work and learn collaboratively on a particular theme or focus and can be run by any interested and qualified persons or group. More specifically, family learning programmes are run by registered family learning tutors; family provision is part of the adult and community learning budget offered by the Learning and Skills Council to local education authorities. Such programmes tend to be literacy or numeracy based. They aim to help parents learn how best to support their child's learning and often include elements of basic skills learning in maths or literacy, along with offering opportunities for parents to study for national tests, although this is not their main focus.

The Pen Green Centre in Corby has been revolutionary in terms of establishing a rigorous and well-respected programme of family involvement and community education. Its work with the community has led them to develop a specific pedagogy described as Parents' Involvement in their Children's Learning (PICL) Programme (Whalley, 2007). This has resulted in staff from many early years settings receiving training to enable them to understand more fully how their work with parents can have not only a positive impact on the learning of the child, but also on the parents and on the community as a whole. This approach is based on four concepts:

- involvement

- well-being

- adult style

- schemas.

Time is devoted to giving parents opportunities to learn about these concepts to enable them to understand more fully about how their child can learn. Through observations of, and discussions with, their own child, they build up a picture of their child as a powerful learner.

 Case study: Two Moors Family Learning Group

Influenced by the Pen Green model of parental involvement, the Family Learning Group at Two Moors Primary School in Devon supports parents in observing their child's play, identifying schemas and building up a portfolio of their child's play and experiences.

During one particular programme, supported by external funding, the group chose the focus 'Mathematical development as observed in young children's play'. Over several weeks, parents of under-4s were encouraged to:

- find out about schemas through tuition with the family learning tutor
- observe and photograph their child play in nursery and engage in mathematical activities with their child
- observe their child's play at home and repeat activities observed and participated in at school
- attend a planned visit to a local forest, supported by tutors, to collect natural materials used to stimulate play and explore repeating patterns
- attend sessions led by the family learning tutor and an early years teacher to discover more about early years mathematics, the place of mathematics in the EYFS and its progression into Key Stage 1
- use information gathered to compile a portfolio about their child's schematic play, highlighting mathematical aspects.

(Continued)

(Continued)

Using their observations, photos and discussions with other members of the group, parents were able to identify their child's schemas and particular mathematical interests. With support from the tutor, they were able to compile portfolios that not only showed their child to be an active and independent learner, but also a competent and emerging mathematician. Parents involved in the programme felt they:

- could more clearly identify aspects of their child's mathematical development in day-to-day routines and play
- were more confident in their use of language to support mathematical development
- could provide play things which best suited their child's individual interests and learning
- had gained some understanding of how mathematics education starts in the early years and progresses into primary school.

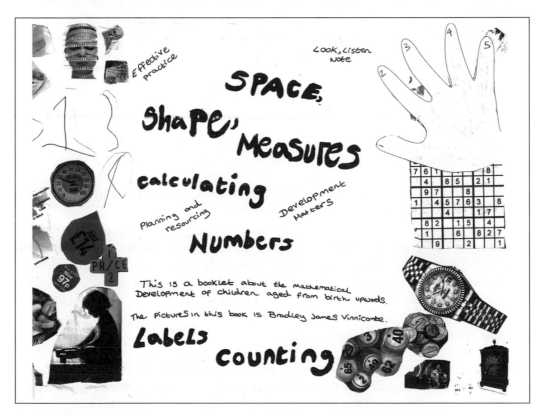

Figure 9.1   Opening page from a parent's Family Learning Group portfolio

Involving parents in playful mathematics

Most importantly, parents need to feel welcome. An atmosphere of friendliness, respect and trust must be established first; if a parent feels uncomfortable coming into a setting or classroom, they are unlikely to repeat the experience. Once parents feel welcome, they will be more receptive to initiatives showing them that mathematics is creative, exciting and to be enjoyed with their child. There are several strategies for involving parents in playful mathematics:

- Make sure that the environment is as light and attractive as possible and that a practitioner is free to talk to parents as they come into the setting or classroom.

- Give parents the opportunity to observe mathematics sessions, ensuring they see a mix of focused teaching and independent playful maths. This will allow them to see how mathematics can be interesting, creative and make connections with other areas of learning and the child's interests. It will also allow parents to become aware of progression as staff talk about the learning that preceded the observed session, and the teaching and learning that will follow. It may also give parents the opportunity to understand more about sustained shared thinking.

- Invite parents to regular storytime sessions during which stories that explore mathematical concepts are read (see Resources). This gives the practitioner the opportunity to model effective practice such as singing counting songs and rhymes, using number lines (see Chapter 4), clapping patterns and modelling a range of mathematical vocabulary.

- Lend maths games, such as board games, pattern-making games, games with clocks.

- Involve parents in making maths story sacks. Local libraries and Children's Centres often have a good supply to lend and which will stimulate ideas.

- Give parents booklets about aspects of mathematics illustrated with photos and examples of children's mathematical graphics.

- Encourage parents to look at displays of mathematical graphics and annotated photos of children engaged in playful mathematics. It is important to indicate whether the photos are of self-initiated or adult-led learning and exactly which mathematical skills the child is learning and practising.

- Hold maths 'story trails' (see below).

- Provide early work which is maths based. Encourage parents to be involved in a maths-based task when the children come into their classroom. Such a task might be to notice how the pattern of harvest fruit on display has changed from the previous day, to hang clothes on a small washing line in a repeating pattern, or to find and record 'hidden number bonds' in a 3D display.

- Encourage the use of a graphics board where children and parents can make mathematical marks collectively. Children and parents are invited to write a response to questions posted on the board such as, 'How many people live in your house?' and 'What is your favourite number?'

Creative ideas for good practice

As a means of encouraging parents to see maths as enjoyable and achievable and to provide a family-friendly way to model mathematical activities, invite parents to a maths story sack workshop:

- Choose a good children's story which offers lots of mathematical potential (see Resources).
- Identify mathematical activities and games suggested by the story such as pattern making, matching number of objects to numerals, making number lines, making price tags and so on.
- Invite parents to join the making workshop and have a sample story sack there for them to see.
- Introduce them to the book and discuss and model all of the mathematical opportunities suggested by the book. Not only does this enable parents to make their own suggestions, but allows them to see mathematical opportunities they otherwise might not have, and raise the mathematical profile of such activities as pattern making and the use of mathematical vocabulary.
- Identify which resources, relevant to the book, are going to be made and how.
- Provide a comfortable and welcoming room where parents can meet and work together over a series of weeks to develop the project.

 Creative ideas for good practice

The mathematical potential of storybooks, and the meaningful connections between literacy and mathematics, can be highlighted by mathematical story trails:

- Choose a book with lots of opportunities for mathematical activities and read to the children and parents (see Resources).
- Take the children and parents on a trail around the school in which you have placed mathematical encounters related to the book. These might include spotting the repeating pattern of clothes hanging on a washing line, finding the longest and shortest broom or the heaviest and the lightest sack of corn.
- Use each encounter to model effective practice.
- Take photos of the trail to annotate and display later to highlight the mathematical potential of the activities encountered.

Dialogue with parents about maths and play

A partnership between parents and teachers can only be established if parents feel their views are both invited and valued. There will be little of a partnership if liaison is based upon the teacher telling the parent 'how it's done'. Real dialogue can be achieved through the family learning opportunities described above, but not exclusively so. This dialogue can also be achieved in any setting or classroom where early years staff are keen to facilitate it. Parents can and should be involved in assessment of their young child's mathematical development. This can be achieved regularly through a variety of strategies:

- Using a 'working wall'. A 'working' or 'observation wall' is a large display board on which practitioners display a mix of dated written observations of the children, or annotated photos (see Activity 6.3). The display acts as a means of celebrating skills and interests the children are currently showing. Parents are also encouraged to pin up observations they have made of their children, or annotated photos, showing significant achievements, such as the first time a child puts on their shoes and socks, or writes their name. This acts as a way of keeping both practitioners and parents regularly informed and, importantly, ensures that parents contribute to the observation, assessment and planning cycle. This will then inform the planning of continuous provision effectively based on children's achievements and interests. While some parents do not like their observations of their child being on display for all to see, they may be more comfortable posting them in an 'observation folder' attached to the wall.

- Making portfolios of children's progress in the Foundation Stage. Using portfolios or 'learning journey' books is also a successful way of involving parents. Displaying annotated photos and mathematical graphics in this way allows parents to see the child engaged in activities they might otherwise be unaware of. Including annotated photos of children engaged in playful mathematics acts to highlight the mathematical content of much of a young child's activity and play. Settings using such portfolios often invite parents to see them regularly. Some include an evaluation or comments sheet for the parents to comment on what they have seen in the portfolio.

- Involving parents in the Early Years Foundation Stage Profile (EYFSP). It is crucial, once the child is in Reception class, that parents are invited regularly to discuss their child's progress and assessment with the teachers, all of which are integral to the EYFSP process. It acts as a way of keeping parents informed and also takes into account their views, once again involving them in the observation, assessment and planning cycle.

- Giving parents questionnaires that invite them to describe their child's interests and skills enables them indirectly to contribute to the planning of continuous provision.

- An 'open door' policy allows parents to bring their child into the setting, look at displays, be involved in early work and have the opportunity to talk to members of staff.

If parents and teachers can share their knowledge about the child's mathematical development, the implications of this dialogue can be far reaching. Not only can the parent and teacher gain new insight into the child as a developing mathematician, but the teacher will then be able to plan and match continuous provision and focused teaching sessions more appropriately. Similarly, parents may discover different ways in which they can support their child through playful activity at home. Most crucially, however, the family can support the child's view of themselves as an eager and able doer of mathematics.

Involving parents checklist

- Do parents feel welcome when they come into the classroom/setting?
- Do all parents feel that their child is included in maths displays and opportunities regardless of their mathematical attainment?
- Is there a range of informative and attractive maths displays to interest parents?
- Are parents able to stand or sit comfortably to read displays, or are the displays situated in a thoroughfare?
- Is there a practitioner available to talk to parents and draw their attention to new maths displays or photos of their child and explain their mathematical significance?
- Are instructions for any early work or the graphics board made clear to all parents?
- Is there an information board to inform parents about maths meetings, family learning courses and other relevant information?
- What opportunities are there for parents to share their observations of their child's mathematical development?
- Are maths story sacks and maths games available in a central place and in a place that will attract parents to them?
- Have all the parents seen recent evidence of their child's engagement in mathematics, either through display or discussion with practitioners?
- Are parents aware of the significance of counting collections, number lines and the graphics area to their child's mathematical development?

Suggested further reading

Athey, C. (1990) *Extending Thought In Young Children: A Parent–Teacher Partnership*. London: Paul Chapman Publishing.

Carruthers, E. and Worthington, M. (2006) *Children's Mathematics: Making Marks, Making Meaning*, 2nd edition. London: Sage Publications.

DCSF (2008) *Independent Review of Mathematics Teaching in Early Years Settings and Primary Schools*. Available at www.publications.teachernet.gov.uk

Desforges, C. (2003) *The Impact of Parental Involvement, Parental Support and Family Education on Pupil Achievement and Adjustment* (Research Report 433). London: DfES.

DfES (2004) *Parents: Partners in Learning, Guidance for Schools*. London: DfES.

Griffiths, R. (2008) 'The family counts' in I. Thompson (ed.) *Teaching and Learning Early Number*, 2nd edition. Berkshire: OUP.

Hutchin, V. (2003) *Observing and Assessing Children's Learning*, 2nd edition. London: David Fulton Publishers.

Whalley, M. (2007) *Involving Parents in their Children's Learning*, 2nd edition. London: Paul Chapman Publishing.

Appendices

Photocopiable 1: Independent play

  Role play	• Learning opportunities and curriculum links • Resources	 *Small world drama*	• Learning opportunities and curriculum links • Resources
  Table-top/pattern making	• Learning opportunities and curriculum links • Resources	 *Reading and listening area*	• Learning opportunities and curriculum links • Resources
  Creative and aesthetic area	• Learning opportunities and curriculum links • Resources	 *Graphics area*	• Learning opportunities and curriculum links • Resources

Mathematics Through Play in the Early Years, Second Edition, © Kate Tucker, 2010. (SAGE)

(Continued)

(Continued)

ICT	• Learning opportunities and curriculum links • Resources
Construction	• Learning opportunities and curriculum links • Resources
Play tray	• Learning opportunities and curriculum links • Resources

Mathematics Through Play in the Early Years, Second Edition, © Kate Tucker, 2010. (SAGE)

Photocopiable 2: Independent play in the outside play area

	Learning opportunities and curriculum links / Resources		Learning opportunities and curriculum links / Resources
Construction	• Learning opportunities and curriculum links • Resources	**PE**	• Learning opportunities and curriculum links • Resources
Role play	• Learning opportunities and curriculum links • Resources	**Play tray/Sandpit**	• Learning opportunities and curriculum links • Resources
Garden/Environment	• Learning opportunities and curriculum links • Resources	**Quiet area**	• Learning opportunities and curriculum links • Resources

Mathematics Through Play in the Early Years, Second Edition, © Kate Tucker. 2010. (SAGE)

Photocopiable 3: Observation sheet for independent play

Date/time	Name	Learning context	Evidence seen of:						Comments
			PSED	CLL	PSRN	KUW	PD	CD	

Mathematics Through Play in the Early Years, Second Edition, © Kate Tucker, 2010. (SAGE)

Photocopiable 4: Record and assessment sheet for review time

Date	Name	Nature of work reviewed	Learning objective addressed

Mathematics Through Play in the Early Years, Second Edition, © Kate Tucker, 2010. (SAGE)

Glossary

Algorithm	A step-by-step procedure for solving a specific problem, such as an addition, subtraction, multiplication or division problem.
Array	An ordered collection of objects or numbers, often presented in rows or columns.
Cardinal	The number that indicates how many there are in a set.
CD	Creative development.
CLL	Communication, language and literacy.
Complementary addition	The mathematical operation that finds out how many more are needed to make a given number.
ELG	Early Learning Goals.
FS	Foundation Stage.
ICT	Information and Communication Technology.
IWB	Interactive whiteboard.
KUW	Knowledge and understanding of the world.
Lit	Literacy.
Ordinal	A number denoting the position in a sequence, such as 1st, 2nd, 3rd, etc.
Partition	The act of dividing a set of objects into two subsets.
PD	Physical development.
PE	Physical Education.
Pictogram	A visual representation of data using pictures to denote the nature of the information it represents.
PNS	Primary National Strategy.
PSRN	Problem solving, reasoning and number.
R	Reception.

RE   Religious Education.

Rotation   The movement of an object about a fixed point.

Schema   Repeated patterns of behaviour in young children.

Sequence   Objects, shapes or numbers arranged in a line, such as cow, sheep, pig. When this is repeated several times, it forms a repeating pattern.

Sukkot   Jewish autumn festival during which families build a three-sided shelter (sukkah) with a roof made of branches and greenery in their garden. It reminds them of the Jews' journey from Egypt to Israel.

Symmetry   A picture or object that has 'sameness' on two sides.

Tessellation Fitting shapes together without leaving gaps.

Translation   Movement along a straight line.

Y1/2   Year 1/2.

Resources

Chapter 1

Mrs Mopple's Washing Line Hewett, Anita (1994) Red Fox

Chapter 2

Jasper's Beanstalk Butterworth, Nick and Inkpen, Mick (1992) Hodder & Stoughton
Bumpus Jumpus Dinosaurumpus Mitton, Tony and Parker-Rees, Guy (2002) Orchard
Ladybird, Ladybird Brown, Ruth (1998) Andersen Press
The Gruffalo Donaldson, Julia and Scheffler, Axel (1999) Macmillan Children's Books
Jamaica and Brianna Havill, Juanita and O'Brien, Anne Sibley (1994) Heinemann
The Sand Horse Turnbull, Ann and Foreman, Michael (2002) Andersen Press
The Enormous Crocodile Dahl, Roald and Blake, Quentin (1978) Cape
Rosie's Walk Hutchins, Pat (1992) Random Century
The Pet Shop Ahlberg, Allan and Amstutz, Andre (1990) Heinemann
A Bit More Bert Ahlberg, Allan and Briggs, Raymond (2002) Puffin
The Mousehole Cat Barber, Antonia and Bayley, Nicola (1990) Walker Books
Handa's Hen Browne, Eileen (2002) Walker Books
Handa's Surprise Browne, Eileen (1994) Walker Books

Chapter 3

The Story of Little Babaji, Bannerman, Helen and Marcellino, Fred (1997) Ragged Bears

Chapter 4

Numicon®, Numicon Limited, www.numicon.com

Useful storybooks depicting counting, cardinal and ordinal number

My Granny Went to Market: A Round the World Counting Book Blackstone, Stella (1995) Barefoot Books
Mr Magnolia Blake, Quentin (1999) Red Fox
Handa's Hen Browne, Eileen (2002) Walker Books
Engines, Engines Bruce, Lisa (2001) Trafalgar Square

1, 2, 3, to the Zoo: A Counting Book Carle, Eric (1987) Hamish Hamilton
Out for the Count Cave, Kathryn (1991) Frances Lincoln Ltd
Ten Green Monsters Clarke, Gus (1993) Andersen Press
One Green Island Hard, Charlotte (1996) Walker Books
Emeka's Gift Oneyefulu, Ifeoma (1995) Frances Lincoln Ltd

Addition and subtraction

Five Little Ducks Beck, Ian (1992) Orchard Books
Ten Seeds Brown, Ruth (2001) Andersen Press
Many Hands Counting Book Granstorm, Brita (1999) Walker Books
Ten Red Apples Miller, Virginia (2002) Walker Books
Ten Terrible Pirates Rogers, Paul and Emma (1994) David Bennett
Two Little Witches Ziefert, Harriet (1996) Walker Books

Using money

A Bargain for Frances Hoban, Russell (1992) Mammoth
The Great Pet Sale Inkpen, Mick (1998) Hodder Children's Books
Small Change Lewis, Rob (1992) Red Fox
Bunny Money Wells, Rosemary (1991) Picture Corgi

Multiplication and division

The Doorbell Rang Hutchins, Pat (1986) Bodley Head
One Is a Snail, Ten Is a Crab Sayre, April Pulley et al. (2003) Walker Books

Chapter 5

Bridget Riley: Paintings from the 60s and 70s texts by Corrin, Lisa G., Kudielka, Robert and Spalding, Frances (1999) Serpentine Gallery
African, Indian and Islamic Art, www.geomatrix.co.uk
Andy Goldsworthy produced by Hollis, Jill and Cameron, Ian (1990) Viking
www.artchive.com/artchive/K/klee.html
www.morrissociety.org
Tom Thumb's Musical Maths MacGregor, Helen (1998) A & C Black

Useful storybooks depicting pattern

What Goes Snap? Boyle, Alison and Gale, Cathy (1998) Walker Books
The Very Hungry Caterpillar Carle, Eric (1970) Hamilton
Kings of Another Country French, Fiona (1992) Oxford University Press
Nikos the Fisherman French, Fiona (1995) Oxford University Press
Mrs Mopple's Washing Line Hewett, Anita (1994) Red Fox
Ten Bright Eyes Hindley, Judy (1998) Leveinson
Lucy and Tom's 1, 2, 3 Hughes, Shirley (1989) Puffin
Curious Clownfish Maddern, Eric (1990) Frances Lincoln

Elmer McKee, David (1990) Red Fox
My Mum and Dad Make Me Laugh Sharratt, Nick (1994) Walker Books

Chapter 6

The Big Concrete Lorry Hughes, Shirley (1989) Walker
Snail Trail Brown, Ruth (2000) Andersen
Traffic Jam Owen, Annie (1990) Orchard Books
Come Away From the Water, Shirley Burningham, John (1977) Cape
Jack's Fantastic Voyage Foreman, Michael (1994) Red Fox
Katie Morag and the Two Grandmothers Hedderwick, Mairi (1985) Bodley Head
Community Playthings, www.communityplaythings.com
Mondrian Deicher, Susanne (2001) Midpoint Press
Barbara Hepworth Gale, Matthew and Stephens, Chris (2001) Tate Gallery
Publishing
Spy Shapes in Art Micklethwait, Lucy (2004) Collins

Useful storybooks showing shape and space

Brown Rabbit's Shape Book Baker, Alan (1994) Kingfisher
If At First You Do Not See Brown, Ruth (1982) Sparrow
The Secret Birthday Message Carle, Eric (1972) Hamish Hamilton
Little Cloud Carle, Eric (1998) Puffin
The Shape of Things Dodds Dale, Ann (1994) Walker
The Wheeling and Whirling-Around Book Hindley, Judy and Chamberlain, Margaret
(1994) Walker
Changes, Changes Hutchins, Pat (1994) Red Fox
Grandfather Tang's Story Tompert, Ann (1991) MacRae
The Shape Game Browne, Anthony (2003) Doubleday

ICT

PIXIE, www.swallow.co.uk
Roamer™, www.valiant-technology.com
Bee-bot, www.tts-group.co.uk

Chapter 7

Lasy®, Lasy® GmbH, info@lasy.com

Useful storybooks about weight and capacity

Who Sank the Boat? Mien, Pamela (1982) Hamilton
The Lighthouse Keeper's Catastrophe Armitage, Ronda and David (1986) Deutsch
Mr Gumpy's Outing Burningham, John (2001) Red Fox
Honey Biscuits Hooper, Meredith (1997) Kingfisher

Length, distance and height

Rosie's Walk Hutchins, Pat (1992) Random Century
Six Feet Long and Three Feet Wide Billington, Jeannie and Smee, Nicola (1999) Walker Books
Jim and the Beanstalk Briggs, Raymond (1970) Hamilton
Hue Boy Mitchell, Rita Phillips (1992) Gollancz

Time

The Bad-Tempered Ladybird Carle, Eric (1997) Hamilton
Tick-Tock Dunbar, James (1996) Franklin Watts
Mr Wolf's Week Hawkins, Colin (1997) Picture Lions
The Stopwatch Lloyd, David (1986) Walker Books
The School Bus Comes at Eight O'Clock McKee, David (1993) Andersen Press

Chapter 8

2Simple Software, info@2simple.com
Bear's Adventure Blathwayt, Benedict (1988) MacRae
The Lighthouse Keeper's Lunch Armitage, Rhonda and David (2007) Scholastic

Useful websites for curriculum, planning and assessment

www.acurriculumforexcellencescotland.gov.uk
www.standards.dcsf.gov.uk
www.teachernet.gov.uk/publications
www.wales.gov.uk/foundationphase
www.childrens-mathematics.net

References

Athey, C. (1990) *Extending Thought in Your Children: A Parent–Teacher Partnership.* London: Paul Chapman Publishing.

Atkinson, S. (ed.) (1992) *Mathematics with Reason. The Emergent Approach to Primary Maths.* London: Hodder & Stoughton.

Bennett. N., Wood, L. and Rogers, S. (1997) *Teaching Through Play: Teacher's Thinking and Classroom Practice.* Buckingham: Open University Press.

Bilton, H. (1998) *Outdoor Play in the Early Years: Management and Innovation.* London: David Fulton Publishers.

Bruce, T. (1991) *Time to Play in Early Childhood Education.* London: Hodder & Stoughton.

Bruner, J. (1991) 'The nature and uses of immaturity', in M. Woodhead. R. Carr and R. Light (eds) *Becoming a Person.* London: Routledge/Open University Press, pp. 247–72.

Burke, S., Slaughter, C. and Tynemouth, A. (eds) (2002) *Play Maths!* Devon: Devon Curriculum Services.

Carruthers, E. and Worthington, M. (2006) *Children's Mathematics: Making Marks, Making Meaning,* 2nd edition. London: Sage Publications.

DCSF (2007) *The Children's Plan: Building Brighter Futures.* Norwich: Her Majestry's Stationery Office.

DCSF (2008) *The Independent Review of Mathematics Teaching in Early Years Settings and Primary Schools.* www.publications.teachers.gov.uk/eOrderingDownload/Williams% 20Mathematics.pdf (accessed June 2008).

Desforges, C. (2003) *The Impact of Parental Involvement, Parental Support and Family Education on Pupil Achievement and Adjustment.* (Research Report 433). London: Department for Education and Schools.

DfEE (1999) *The National Numeracy Strategy.* London: Department for Education and Employment.

DfES (2002) *Birth to Three Matters: A Framework to Support Children in their Earliest Years.* London: Department for Education and Skills.

DfES (2006) *Primary Framework for Literacy and Mathematics.* Norwich: Department for Education and Skills.

DfES (2007a) *Statutory Framework for the Early Years Foundation Stage.* Nottingham: Department for Education and Skills.

DfES (2007b) *Practice Guidance for the Early Years Foundation Stage.* Nottingham: Department for Education and Skills.

Donaldson, M. (1978) *Children's Minds.* Glasgow: Fontana.

Fawcett, M. (2002) A non-paginated discussion paper 'Creativity in the early years: children as "authors and inventors"', *Early Education* (38), autumn.

Fisher, J. (2002) *Starting from the Child.* Buckingham: Open University Press.

Gersten, N., Jordan, C. and Flojo, J.R. (2005) 'Early identification and interventions for students with mathematics difficulties', *Journal of Learning Disabilities,* 38(4): 293–304.

Gifford, S. (2008) '"How do you teach nursery children mathematics?" In search of a mathematics pedagogy for the early years', in I. Thompson (ed.) *Teaching and Learning Early Number,* 2nd edition. Berkshire: Open University Press, pp. 217–26.

Griffiths, R. (1994) 'Mathematics and Play', in J.R. Moyles (ed.) *The Excellence of Play*. Buckingham: Open University Press, pp. 145–47.

Gura, R. (ed.) (1992) *Exploring Learning: Young Children and Blockplay*. London: Paul Chapman Publishing.

Haylock, D. and Cockburn, A. (2003) *Understanding Mathematics in the Lower Primary Years*. London: Paul Chapman Publishing.

Hughes, M. (1986) *Children and Number*. Oxford: Basil Blackwell.

Kitson, N. (1994) '"Please Miss Alexander: will you be the robber?" Fantasy Play: a case for adult intervention', in J.R. Moyles (ed.) *The Excellence of Play*. Buckingham: Open University Press, pp. 88–98.

Lindon, J. (2001) *Understanding Children's Play*. Cheltenham: Nelson Thornes.

Montague-Smith, A. (2002) *Mathematics in Nursery Education*. London: David Fulton Publishers.

Moyles, J.R. (ed.) (1994) *The Excellence of Play*. Buckingham: Open University Press.

National Advisory Committee on Creativity and Cultural Education (NACCCE) (1999) *All Our Futures: Creativity, Culture and Education*. Department for Education and Employment/Department for Culture, Media and Sport.

Ofsted (2004) *Transition for the Reception Year to Year 1: An Evaluation by HMI*. London: Officer for Standards in Education.

Ouvry, M. (2003) *Exercising Muscles and Minds: Outdoor Play and the Early Years Curriculum*. London: National Children's Bureau.

Pound, L. (1999) *Supporting Mathematical Development in the Early Years*. Buckingham: Open University Press.

Qualifications and Curriculum Authority (QCA) (2000) *Curriculum Guidance for the Foundation Stage*. London: Qualifications and Curriculum Authority.

Rhydderch-Evans, Z. (1993) *Mathematics in the School Grounds*. Devon: Southgate Publishers.

Rogers, S. and Evans, J. (2008) *Inside Role Play in Early Childhood Education*. London: Routledge.

Rogers, S. and Tucker, K. (2003) 'Mind travel', *Primary Geography* 51(April): 13–14.

Rose, J. (2009) *Independent Review of the Primary Curriculum: Final Report*. Publications. teachernet.gov.uk/eOrderingDownload/Primary_curriculum_Report.pdf (accessed May 2009).

SE (2007) *A curriculum for excellence: Building the curriculum 2. Active Learning in the Early Years*. www.ltscotland.org.uk/Images/Building%20the%20Curriculum%202tcm4-408069.pdf (accessed May 2009).

Siraj-Blatchford, I., Silva, K., Mutlock, S., Gilden, R. and Bell, D. (2002) *Researching Effective Pedagogy in the Early Years* (Research Report 356). London: Department for Education and Skills.

Tucker, K. (2001a) 'An interactive approach to learn about maths', *Early Years Educator* 3(7), November, 15–17.

Tucker, K. (2001b) 'Jumping on to a good idea to teach maths', *Early Years Educator* 3(3), July, 18–20.

Tucker, K. (2002a) 'You can count on drama to teach maths skills', *Early Years Educator* 3(9), January, 13–18.

Tucker, K. (2002b) 'Stretch children's imagination a little bit further', *Early Years Educator* 4(7), November, 32–5.

Tucker, K. (2003) 'Mathematical development in the early years', *Early Years Educator* 4(10), February, ii–viii.

Vygotsky, L.S. (1978) *Mind in Society,* translated and edited by M. Cole, V. John-Steiner, S. Scribner and E. Souberman. Cambridge, MA: Harvard University Press.

WAG (2008) *Framework for Children's Learning for 3- to 7-year-olds in Wales.* Cardiff: Welsh Assembly Government.

Whalley, M. (2007) *Involving Parents in their Children's Learning,* 2nd edition. London: Paul Chapman Publishing.

Worthington, M. and Carruthers, E. (2003) *Children's Mathematics: Making Marks, Making Meaning.* London: Paul Chapman Publishing.

Index

Added to a page number 'f' denotes a figure and 't' denotes a table.
Entries in bold refer to activities.